THE QUANTUM ADVANTAGE
A New Leadership Guide for Business Managers

About the Author

MARK B. STEWART has spent the last thirty years as a corporate executive leader. Currently, Stewart is Senior Vice President of Wireline Operations at Intrado, Inc. in Longmont, Colorado. Founded in 1979, Intrado Inc. is pioneering the technology of Informed Response® by providing telecommunications companies and public safety organizations with accurate, efficiently delivered, mission-critical information. Prior to joining Intrado, Stewart was the CEO of iAccess Communications, a start-up telecommunications services company in Denver, Colorado, that provides technical telecommunications services and advanced leadership consulting. He was formerly an executive at US WEST, Inc., a large telecommunications carrier serving the mountain west. Throughout his career, Stewart has focused on creating leadership models that create value for his company with a focus on people. Stewart received his MA from the University of Denver in Denver, Colorado. He resides with is wife Terri and their five children in Parker, Colorado.

The Quantum Advantage

A New Leadership Guide for Business Managers

MARK B. STEWART

BLACKHALL
Publishing

This book was typeset by
ASHFIELD PRESS PUBLISHING SERVICES
for

BLACKHALL PUBLISHING
27 Carysfort Avenue
Blackrock
Co. Dublin
Ireland

e-mail: blackhall@eircom.net
www.blackhallpublishing.com

ISBN: 1 842180 49 5

A catalogue record for this book is available from the British Library.

Printed in Ireland by
ColourBooks Ltd

Contents

SECTION II: THE DESTINATION

Introduction

SEARCHING FOR THE PASSIONATE LEADER IN US

The next time you have the opportunity to pass by the open door of a conference room containing another corporate meeting—an assembly of the eager team members poised to solve yet another corporate conundrum—look at their faces. Stop for a moment, pause, and allow the image to smolder in your mind. Can you hear the hum of the projector—displaying its pictures one after another in monotony only disturbed by the occasional flash of the laser pointer? You can see someone speaking but you cannot hear the words; your mind refuses to participate in such uninspiring dissertation. Before you move on, relieved that it is not you in there, you ask yourself some questions: Where is the energy? Why is there no passion for the work evident when two or more people gather in the name of the company? You may even ask yourself who is leading this bunch—who is taking ownership to insure an atmosphere of energy, passion, and creativity.

Perhaps your mind wanders a bit and your imagination takes over. You conjure up a different image; an image of teams and members of teams working in a synchronous motion—everyone active and everyone engaged—the energy is so thick in the air you'd swear you could feel its tingle on your skin. You can see no end to the flow of creative ideas. Everyone is engaged in meaningful work and they know how their efforts contribute to the mission and vision of the company. All are sharing; they are sharing their time—they are sharing of themselves. You can feel the confidence surging through the team. You know as they know that defeat is not a part of their vocabulary. The teams know that sometimes they may fail in their attempts—but they will never surrender to failure. Again, you take the time to notice their faces.

We are all in search of a better way to lead people and a better way to follow. We are searching for those key ingredients that will build the foundation of our new leadership model. Most of us have experienced the dull and draining meeting that not only fails to energize us but also succeeds in sapping what little energy we have left. We look to our leaders for answers, but all we get in return are blank stares and sympathetic sighs, and an over-used call to continue to do more with less. We go on to ask ourselves "is this all there is?" Why does it continue to take more and more effort to produce lesser results? Where are all the good new ideas going to come from? Why am I so unhappy in my work?

SCIENCE CAN HELP US IN OUR SEARCH

First, let me say that this is not a book about science. However, having said that, new scientific discoveries of the 20th century will figure significantly in our efforts to redefine ourselves as the new leaders of the 21st century and this new science will help us build a new leadership model. You will not find in-depth discussions and accounts of these new scientific theories in this work—plenty of good books have been written already that do a marvelous job of explaining all the theories. What you will find in this book concerns developments in the field of quantum physics and chaos and complexity theory coupled with the application of these scientific principles in the real-life business world—the first element in our new model for leadership we call *The Quantum Organization*.

For several centuries, the world has viewed itself through the mechanistic filters defined for us by the science of Sir Isaac Newton. Newton was born in England in 1642 the son of a farmer. Showing an avid interest and some aptitude for mathematics, Newton was sent to Trinity College in Cambridge for his education. It was during his time in Cambridge that most of his theories were developed.

The value of Isaac Newton's contributions to mathematics and science is indisputable—it is obvious that Newton was a genius. Newton described the universe as a vast empty space, a vessel containing innumerable independent objects all constructed of the same material—common atomic building blocks. In this more machine-like vision of the universe, atomic particles are seen as solid in nature, indestructible, and independent one from another. Truly in this version of the cosmos the whole is never greater than the sum of the parts—like a machine—a car for instance. Taking into account the variance in manufacturing the similar parts that make up any ordinary model of automobile are not different one from another. Simply put, the parts are interchangeable, and add no real additional or unique value than the part replaced.

This model of the universe has held a prominent position in the mind of scientists since the 17th century—until the likes of Albert Einstein, Werner Heisenberg, and Niels Bohr came onto the scene in the early 20th century. These great men along with other brilliant men and women have uncovered a most startling picture of the universe.

They discovered that the universe is not made up of discrete solid parts, indestructible and otherwise not connected. The universe is no longer seen as a vast empty space, but it is filled with electromagnetic fields that exert great influence upon all elements—including human beings.

The renowned physicist and philosopher Fritjof Capra tells us:

> The Universe is no longer seen as a machine, made up of a multitude of objects, but has to be pictured as one indivisible, dynamic whole whose parts are essentially interrelated and can be understood only as patterns of a cosmic process.[1]

As we shall see, it is this interconnected nature of the universe that forms the first of three foundational ingredients of our new leadership model and gives us the tools and techniques to bring the model to life. Science helps us understand the interrelated nature of people. It helps us to see that we are more than unenlightened machine parts in an otherwise hierarchical command-and-control world.

OUR SEARCH CONTINUES IN THE HUMAN MIND

The second key element of our leadership model begins in the human mind. Dennis R. Deaton, author of *The Book on Mind Management*, tells us that:

> Human behavior is an effect: Human thought is the cause. Whatever you do, you do first in your mind. Your mind, the ultimate source of all your actions and reactions, orchestrates every deed, performs every act, authors every word.[2]

The mind is the engine of our new leadership model. If Dr. Deaton is correct and the mind is the source of all our actions and all of our creations, then it stands to reason that a focus on tuning this engine is critical to accomplishment and to our leadership success. This means understanding how the mind works and bringing to bear the power and capabilities of both the conscious and subconscious mind.

Scientists tell us much about the subconscious mind. We now know that the subconscious mind works much like a computer in terms of how it manages and accomplishes tasks. In other words, we can give

1. Fritjof Capra, *The Turning Point*, Bantam Books, 1988.
2. Dennis R. Deaton, *The Book on Mind Management*, MMI Publishing, 1996.

our other-than-conscious mind tasks to accomplish and it will work in the background to deliver us solutions.

We also know that the subconscious mind is a vast repository of data—all the information, pictures, books, and conversations we have experienced are stored in our other-than-conscious mind. This information may not always be readily accessible to the conscious mind, but it is always online to our subconscious computer.

If we include the entire mind in a holistic approach to leadership, we can regularly unleash seldom—before experienced creativity in our relationship building, our ideation, and our learning—in short our leadership.

IN SEARCH OF KNOWLEDGE—THE FINAL INGREDIENT

The final ingredient of our leadership model is knowledge—the body of truths and facts accumulated over time—the sum of what we know combined with our experiences. If the mind is our engine then knowledge and information fuels our leadership model.

The Institute for the Learning Sciences (ILS) at Northwestern University was founded in 1989 as an interdisciplinary research and development center dedicated to applying principles of cognitive science, computer science, artificial intelligence, and educational theory to improving the way people learn. The ILS tells us:

> Perhaps the most harmful misconception people have about intelligence is that being smart comes from knowing a lot of rules. Behind this notion is the sense that reading a lot of textbooks and absorbing what they say will lead one to become an expert...While it does make sense to say that intelligence comes from knowledge, most of that knowledge looks quite a bit different than what you find in a textbook.
>
> The world is too complex a place to be adequately characterized by the theories we develop, and for the most part, we know this. Our rules may be useful for the most common situations we encounter, but we cannot help but encounter many situations, which violate or are outside the bounds of the generalizations we make. Having a broad, well-indexed set of cases is what differentiates the expert from the textbook-trained novice. Or, to put another way, being educated means, in its deepest sense, having access to a wealth of cases from which to generalize.[3]

The Quantum Advantage provides real implementations of these new scientific and leadership principles. While we necessarily do not lay

3. The Institute for the Learning Sciences, Northwestern University, 1994.

claim to inventing the name, we will refer to these principles as we have put them into action as *The Quantum Organization.* Most, if not all, of the books touching on the topic of leadership and the new sciences are steeped in theory with little or no practical application. These theoretical books are superior works and they form the foundation for the practical implementations of these theories that will be discussed later. However, these theories are new and they run counter to what we have been taught as true most of our lives. Experiencing a real example is crucial to absolute understanding of these principles[4] and the ability to exchange the old paradigms for the new.

SUMMARY

The Olympics were back on US soil in Salt lake City in 2002 and the world got an up close and personal look at an America steeled with resolve after the unthinkable events of September 11, 2001, mired in an economic down turn, and yet full of hope and eager for a new brand of heroes to emerge from these games. These heroes came in the form of:

- Snowboarder Chris Klug, who won a bronze medal after enduring a life threatening liver transplant.
- We rejoiced, as Vonetta Flowers became the first black person to win an Olympic Winter Games gold medal.
- And how will we ever forget how we felt as we witnessed Jim Shea's (Jr.) glide to victory in the skeleton accompanied by a picture of his recently deceased grandfather.

So it is in business, we too are ready for a new brand of leader–someone that can bring passion and energy back into the workplace. We are looking for a leader that truly sees the value in people and knows that the power to become this new brand of leader is within reach. We can become that leader and we can help others to see our vision; we have new scientific knowledge and supporting tools that will unlock the true potential within us, we have the untapped powers of our mind, and we have knowledge–knowledge we can grow on a daily basis.

  In closing, the words of William Jennings Bryan provide us a mov-

---

4. All of the quantum principles identified in this book are organized into the following three disciplines:
   1. Synchronizing with our True Nature–Understanding the Science of our Times.
   2. Applying the Full Power of the Mind–Including the Subconscious.
   3. Attaining and Applying Knowledge.

ing call to action—a compelling push for us to take control of our lives—to become masters of our own destiny:

> To be used for a purpose recognized by yourself as a mighty one. To be a force of nature rather than a feverish selfish little clod of ailments and grievances complaining that the world will not devote itself to making me happy. I am of the opinion that my life belongs to the whole community. And as long as I live, it is my privilege to do for it whatever I can. I want to be thoroughly used up when I die; for the harder I work the more that I live. I rejoice in life for its own sake. Life is no brief candle to me, its a sort of splendid torch that I've got to hold up for the moment and I want to make it burn as brightly as possible before handing it on to future generations.

The Journey

Chapter 1

A Vision:
The Key to Increasing Human Productivity

THERE is nothing more disenchanting to man than to be shown the springs and mechanism of any art. All our arts and occupations lie wholly on the surface; it is on the surface that we perceive their beauty, fitness, and significance; and to pry below is to be appalled by their emptiness and shocked by the coarseness of the strings and pulleys.[1]

INTRODUCTION

Current organizational structures not only fail to bring out the best in people, but they also tend to hinder individuals from working at their full potential. The principles upon which today's organizational sciences are built were conceived as far back as the 17th century. In order to reach our full potential, we must build leadership models based on the principles and the scientific revelations of our time.

Due to today's outdated organizational structures and tired leadership models employers are not able to take advantage of an employee's full potential. Imagine the dramatic impact on the workplace, the community and even on the world if we could achieve even 20 percent improvement in effective real work.

In his 1999 study comparing work practices and their effect on employee turnover and productivity, James P. Guthrie tells us that employee-focused policies, what he calls High Involvement Work Practices (HIWP), increase employee retention and drive significant productivity. According to Guthrie, among others these HIWP include: creative use of training, training focused on future skill requirements, allowing more employee participation, information sharing, use of teams, and asking employees how they feel (attitudinal surveys).

---

1. Robert Louis Stevenson (1889) *Art of Writing.*

Guthrie's findings indicate that companies can increase their overall productivity (measured as average revenue per employee) as much as 30 percent or more, with similar improvement in employee retention.[2]

This book was written for corporate managers looking for a new way to lead. This is not a book about how to pinch more work out of people for less—the appalling watchwords for today's unenlightened leaders. This book focuses on delivering real corporate worth by "driving shareholder value." It is my contention that the famous, perhaps infamous, company mission statement of "driving shareholder value" may be the greatest roadblock to real value in corporate America. In today's world there is ample evidence that corporate CEOs tend to choose thoughtless policies that they hope will drive shareholder value, such as employee downsizing, that in fact do just the opposite.

This book was written for those concerned managers who are uneasy with downsizing policies aimed just at boosting stock price. As managers, we know that the true principles that underpin value are steeped in the import of the human asset. Today's shortsighted corporate "right-sizing" policies are just wrong and will cripple our ability to drive real, tangible, long-term value.

Wayne F. Cascio, a noted researcher and scholar on the topic of downsizing, indicates that his research confirms what we believe; that there is a better alternative to indiscriminate downsizing:

> Downsizing, the planned elimination of positions or jobs, is a phenomenon that has affected hundreds of companies and millions of workers since the late 1980s...In many firms the anticipated economic benefits fail to materialize. Examples of these are lower expense ratios, higher profits and increased return-on-investment, and boosted stock prices. Likewise, many anticipated organizational benefits do not develop. These include lower overhead, smoother communications, greater entrepreneurship, and increases in productivity. To a large extent, this is a result of a failure to break out of the traditional approach to organization design and management—an approach founded on the principles of command, control, and compartmentalization.[3]

This book delivers real alternatives to slashing headcounts founded on principles of inventiveness, growth, efficiency, and creating real value.

In this book, you will learn:

1. Effective new leadership tools.

2. James P. Guthrie (1999) "High Involvement Work Practices, Turnover and Productivity," *Academy of Management Journal*, Vol. 1, pp. 180–90.
3. Wayne F. Cascio (1993) "Downsizing: What Do We Know? What Have We Learned?" *Academy of Management Executive*, Vol. 7, No. 1, pp. 94–104.

2. How to design effective organizations.
3. How to tap into employees' hidden capacity.
4. How to increase employee productivity.
5. A new and powerful leadership model.

You will discover compelling principles derived from fresh scientific discoveries about how the universe and nature function. We, the individuals, are essential participants in this dance of life. Synchronizing humanity and nature (synchronicity)[4] is important in order to ensure harmony, happiness, and accomplishment—all indispensable ingredients in this work of art we call life. The fundamental principle in all of the theories[5] addressing leadership and science is that synchronizing what we do and how we do it with our true nature delivers greater efficiency. By way of example, a gasoline engine gives us a metaphor for synchronicity and efficiency. Like people, the gasoline engine is most efficient when all aspects and all components of the engine are finely tuned and synchronized one with another. Only when we truly understand the theory behind combustion engines can we synchronize the delivery of fuel and air, the firing of the spark plugs, and the alignment of the transmission and axels to fire the motor and create motive power.

This work is singular because it provides real examples of these new scientific and leadership principles in action. All of the books touching on the topic of leadership and the new sciences provide us the theories that are applied in this book. These theoretical books are superior works, and they form the foundation for the examples that will be presented later in this book. However, the theories in these books are new, and they run counter to what we have been taught as true most of our lives. Therefore, experiencing a real example is crucial to our absolute understanding of these new principles and our ability to exchange the old paradigms for the new.

In Section I we will build a vision for our new leadership model—*The Quantum Organization*. This vision will act as the blueprint for our new organizational design and leadership style. We will examine some of the recent scientific principles that form the basis for our new thinking. In Section II we will reveal how these new techniques work in the real world—in the corporate world. Finally, we will summarize what we have learned, what we have become, and what we have yet to achieve.

Fasten your seatbelts: You are in for the leadership ride of your life!

---

4. Synchronicity is defined by Webster as the act of being synchronous.
5. See chapter 7 for a short list of books that discuss synchronicity—synchronizing humanity with nature. See also the bibliography.

THE HUMAN FACTOR

For most of my professional life, it was drilled into me that our humanness was a distinct weakness. The term "human error" was an indication that people make mistakes and that those mistakes could not be tolerated—simply put, people needed to be more like machines. Machines do not make mistakes, we were told. When the machine breaks, you simply take it out of service and you fix it. Perhaps the most pejorative concept of all was that when the machine was obsolete you discarded it for a new model. To cast off people in the same way is wrong and, as we shall soon learn, counter productive.

As I watched people struggle within the insensitive bosom of time-honored corporate management styles, it became increasingly clear to me that the traditional leadership techniques I had learned during my 30-plus years in the workplace were just not effective. I could sense that there was a better way. I saw too much inefficiency and waste, conflict, and confusion. I could feel in my heart that our humanness was not a weakness but rather the key to our success and a better return on human capital.

In early 1998, my good friend John Kelley[6] introduced me to a book, *Synchronicity: The Inner Path of Leadership*, by Joseph Jaworski, that started me on a course of study that has changed my life and my opinion about core leadership principles. I knew I had set out on a mission to make a difference in my little corner of the world.

In my opinion, *Synchronicity* is not the definitive work on the topic of leadership for the 21st century. However, this book stirred my soul at a time when I was struggling with my own style of leadership. I owe a debt of gratitude to Jaworski and his insights, and to Kelley for introducing me to the book.

My introduction to the book occurred when Kelley and I were on a long business flight in early 1998. He had just finished *Synchronicity* and passed it along to me with a passionate recommendation. I put down my own reading and perused the table of contents and the introduction to get the general picture of the subject. Within minutes, I came across the following passage:

> Leadership is about creating a domain in which human beings continually deepen their understanding of reality and become more capable of participating in the unfolding of the world. Ultimately, leadership is about creating new realities.[7]

6. Currently, John Kelley is the President and CEO of McData Corporation in Denver, Colorado.
7. Joseph Jaworski (1996) *Synchronicity: The Inner Path of Leadership*, Berrett-Koehler, Introduction.

When I read this quote, I knew I was on to something. This paragraph resonated with me so soundly that it literally shook me at my very core. These two sentences helped me put words and a vision around what I was feeling about leadership, human relationships, individual accountability, and sharing in the creation of the future.

After our business trip, after I had returned home, as I continued to read the book a concept began to take shape. I ran across a mission statement by noted author Stephen R. Covey that began to make some sense to me. I took a few moments to jot down some thoughts *vis-à-vis* a corporate mission statement. Here is some of my early thinking, sprinkled with some of Covey's work on mission statements:

Our mission is to create value in the lives of our customers and our employees. This means that we create and offer products that make life simpler for our customers, which solve customer problems, and return good economic value to the company.

We will be good managers of this business and exercise good judgment, discernment, and a sense of stewardship about all stakeholders, especially those who have a stake in the welfare or the success of the enterprise. These include investors, suppliers, distributors, dealers, the community, and, above all, our customers, whom we recognize as the key to our success.

We will treat our customers, our employees, and our external relationships with the utmost respect. Our reputation in the community will be of the highest order. We will be honest and true to our values. We will put people first in every situation. We will look for every opportunity to make the world a better place as a result of our being here.

We commit to give our employees a sense of being accepted and a place where they can join with others in common enterprise—to create a challenging work experience in which they can grow and develop. We will give them an opportunity for purpose and meaning in their lives—for making a contribution to that which is meaningful. We do all this with a sense of fairness, justice, equity, and balance.[8]

I knew that these new principles I had been studying were true and correct. I really began to feel good about how things were evolving. I knew that I wanted to be part of an organization that really was

8. My thanks to Stephen R. Covey and some of his thinking on the topic of mission statements.

committed to a mission statement like the one above. Little did I know that my studies over the next four years would take me to a place "where no one has ever been before."

TAPPING INTO THE HUMAN POTENTIAL

My thinking began to crystallize a bit more over the next year. I spent some time with Dr. Anthony Ipsaro, a recognized expert in organizational behavior, who has had great success in creating greater productivity in the workplace. Together we began to explore topics surrounding the barriers that block people from bringing their "whole self" to the workplace. What we discovered was that corporate policies, procedures, prejudices, and those "unwritten rules" we have all heard so much about prevent all of us from bringing all that we are to the corporate table.

So what do we mean when we say, "bring your whole self" to the workplace, or anyplace for that matter? Time and time again, I observed in the workplace managers saying things like, "Leave your personal problems at home," or the over-used, "Don't mix your professional life and your personal life." A recent article in *The Denver Post* by columnist Chuck Green had criticized employees of the local telephone company for bringing pictures of their families to work to share with co-workers and wasting time around the water cooler. Here was just another example of the world telling employees to "check your personal lives at the door before you come into the workplace."[9]

I saw that there was something off beam when the things that matter most to people were not appreciated in the workplace. What does that say about my values and me? Sure, sometimes companies try to say the right things. We see corporate goals and mission statements that include words about valuing people and that people are our greatest asset. Nevertheless, when it comes to matching actions with words, companies usually are left wanting.

Many, if not most, corporate employees run households, raise children, manage budgets, facilitate family disagreements, manage a full calendar, and make strategic decisions day in and day out. Some have part-time jobs in communications, the military, retail, religion, the arts, and more. In their personal lives, employees are often engaged in hobbies that include the performing arts, other fields of study, competitive sports, creative handicrafts, counseling, and so on. The immense value of tapping into this vast variety of talents, skills, and

9. Mr. Green apparently feels that the telephone company still maintains some monopoly status, which makes it a governmental agency and subject to taxpayer scrutiny.

experiences was beginning to become clear to me. With Dr. Ipsaro's help I was visualizing the opportunities that were being lost by not allowing people to bring their whole selves to work.

I was excited about the journey so far. Several great and significant concepts were echoing within me in powerful ways. As with our metaphor of the engine, it is critical to being able to finely tune the human engine to understand clearly the theories and concepts underpinning how nature works and how people fit into nature. Now it was time to unearth the science behind all of this to understand more clearly how to synchronize with our true character.

THE SCIENCE OF LEADERSHIP

It was during this course of study that I happened upon a business acquaintance of mine, Ron Hubert, from the consulting firm of Deloitte and Touche. My path had crossed Ron's a year earlier when he and his colleagues were doing some corporate strategy work for me. The strategy work that was done was excellent. It framed the mechanics of business strategy in some very compelling terms.

While I really was impressed with Ron and his team's work, it was beginning to become clear to me that a missing component in all the strategy work we completed was a segment on human strategy. I mean human strategy in the sense of the power of the individual to create the future, strategies to make possible the unleashing of the power of the subconscious mind, and an organizational theory that can be put in place that is synchronized with the forces of nature.

Ron introduced me to several electrifying new theories: complexity, chaos, and quantum physics. These new theories resonated with me in a profound way. The new sciences provided the intellectual foundation for many of the concepts I had been thinking about:

- Viewing people in a holistic way.
- Building leadership on a foundation of relationships.
- The value of having everyone participate.
- A more ordered and harmonious workplace.
- The absolute value of human creativity.

In her book *Leadership and the New Science*, Margaret J. Wheatley says:

> Each of us lives and works in organizations designed from Newtonian images of the universe...But the science has changed. If we are to continue to draw from the sciences to create and manage organizations,

then we need to at least ground our work in the science of our times. We need to stop seeking after the universe of the Seventeenth Century and begin to explore what became known to us in the Twentieth Century.[10]

Wheatley says that the science of Sir Isaac Newton was a science of the machine. Newton supposed that the universe operates like a machine. Each component—planet, organism, microscopic element—is part of one great machine. If one part fails, you simply fix or replace it with little or no lasting impact to the system as a whole. In other words, there is no connection within and between nature and her elements. Newton essentially says that all the bodies of the universe are analogous to "tinker toy" creations suspended in an otherwise empty universe. The new science, the science of the quantum, says otherwise.[11]

Quantum theory at its essence says that our make-up is of a more connected nature. There are fields of energy flooding the entire universe. These fields, as Wheatley says, are responsible for "action-at-a-distance."[12] Scientists now believe that these fields of energy contain all the information that has ever existed, exists now, or will ever exist in the future. This data is available and influences our lives daily. We are virtually "always online" to God, nature, and the universe.

At the sub-atomic level of the universe, and, therefore, at the very core of human make-up, the physical nature of the universe is a dance of energy. We are made up of the same light and energy as the electro-magnetic fields that permeate space and all of creation. Therefore, it stands to reason that, as a part of this celestial dance, we can have access to nature's wealth of information, and we can be influenced by it. So, the question is, if we can be influenced by this vast collection of energy and knowledge, can we tap into this cosmic database and perhaps even influence it as well?

Another science discipline that comes into play in the new leadership vision is complexity. I was first introduced to the topic through Mitchell Waldrop's book, *Complexity: The Emerging Science at the Edge of Order and Chaos*. The definition of complexity is difficult to get one's arms around.

Complex systems have somehow acquired the ability to bring order and chaos into a special kind of balance. This balance point—often

10. Margaret J. Wheatley (1999) *Leadership and the New Science*, Berrett-Koehler.
11. For further discussion on quantum theory, I recommend either Gary Zukov (1980) *The Dancing Wu Li Masters*, Bantam Books, or John Gribbin (1984) *In Search of Schrodinger's Cat*, Bantam Books.
12. Action-at-a-distance is a phenomenon that describes synchronized actions between human beings or elements that are some distance apart with no apparent mechanism for communication.

called the edge of chaos—is where the components of a system never quite lock into place, and yet never quite dissolve into turbulence, either. The edge of chaos is where life has enough stability to sustain itself and enough creativity to deserve the name of life. The edge of chaos is where new ideas and innovative genotypes are forever nibbling away at the edges of the status quo, and where even the most entrenched old guard will eventually be overthrown.[13]

What a marvelous picture this paints in the fertile mind of the learner. Waldrop continues:

> The edge of chaos is the constantly shifting battle zone between stagnation and anarchy, the one place where a complex system can be spontaneous, adaptive, and alive.[14]

Complexity science introduces us to the concept of strange attractors. Strange attractor is the name scientists have affixed to those few fundamental principles that drive complex systems. Rather than managing all the myriad possibilities of events and relationships in our lives from the top down, the details will take care of themselves if we attend to foundational principles.

For example, Craig Reynolds gives us tremendous insight into the power of managing complex systems. He has designed and programmed software that demonstrates how a complex system can be managed and controlled from the bottom up. He uses flocking birds; he refers to them as boids, flying in a three-dimensional space interacting with trees, buildings, and other impediments. Reynolds programs the boids with three simple rules:

1. The boids must at all times maintain a minimum distance from all other objects, including the other boids.
2. Each boid must approximate the same flying speed of nearby boids.
3. Each boid must at all times attempt to fly to the center of the main body of the flock.

This program demonstrates some very amazing natural behavior:

1. If several boids are released into the space at random intervals,

13. Mitchell Waldrop (1993) *Complexity: The Emerging Science at the Edge of Order and Chaos*, Simon and Schuster, p. 12.
14. Ibid.

they will flock. Simply put, they will find each other and form a group.

2. They will fly around objects put into their path, such as trees and buildings. Once the object is behind them, they re-form the flock.

This is a very vivid example of how complex systems behave and therefore can be controlled or managed. If Reynolds attempted to program each boid with all the unique events or objects it might encounter and all of the correct responses possible, he would still be working on this program—he would still be working on it when his grandchildren graduate college![15]

Christianity gives us an equally compelling example of the wisdom in managing complex systems from the bottom up. In the Bible, we read of Jesus Christ dialoging with the Sadducees and Pharisees regarding the greatest commandments:

> Master, which [is] the great commandment in the law? Jesus said unto him, Thou shalt love the Lord thy God with all thy heart, and with all thy soul, and with all thy mind. This is the first and great commandment. And the second [is] like unto it, Thou shalt love thy neighbor as thyself. On these two commandments hang all the law and the prophets.[16]

We are drawn to the apparent absurdity of an immense and complex religion such as Christianity being grounded to two simple rules. If we try to contemplate the myriad dos and don'ts of this creed, and then complicate this even more by introducing millions upon millions of unique people throughout the ages instructed to model every aspect of their lives after this doctrine, we get a small sense of how complex a system this is. Yet it is impossible to find any tenet of this religion that cannot find its origin and governance in at least one of the two foundational commandments.

THE ENGINE WE CALL THE HUMAN MIND

In 1998, I engaged a learning company with some unique thinking in the area of human productivity. Quma Learning, based in Phoenix, Arizona, advocates that the unconscious mind is perhaps the last great untapped resource. In sum, Quma Learning maintains that the concept of bringing the whole person to the table applied not only to the

15. http://www.red3d.com/cwr/boids/, last accessed March 2002.
16. *The Bible*, King James Version, Matthew, 22: 36–40.

diverse skills, talents, and vast life experiences of the individual, but to the individual's whole mind as well.

We are all on pretty familiar terms with our conscious mind. We spend every waking moment using this great tool in all that we do. We call upon our conscious mind to interpret meaning in what we see, smell, hear, taste, and touch—our conscious mind is our constant companion. We know that the brain is very efficient—conserving energy and resources where possible to be used for other activities. A study conducted in 2000 provides some discerning evidence of the complexity and amazing power of the human brain:

> Using functional MRI, a German University has shown that when learning a motor movement (in this case learning to play the piano), a great deal of the motor region of the brain is used. With experience, smaller and smaller regions of the brain are used. In professional musicians, only very tiny regions of the motor cortex are involved in their playing. Thus, practice makes neural networks efficient and frees up regions of the cortex again to be used for other things.[17]

Dr. Dennis R. Deaton, Chairman of the Board of Quma Learning, makes an astonishing revelation in *The Book on Mind Management.*

> We think, and with those thoughts, we create. We create the world we live in. It goes beyond influencing, shaping or guiding. You and I, in very literal terms, determine what we experience and what we enact into the world...We harvest in life, only and exactly, what we sow in our minds.[18]

Researchers are giving us new insights into the workings of the subconscious mind as well. It is well-known that the other-than-conscious mind controls our breathing, circulation, and digestion—our autonomic system. We know that our memory, emotions, symbolic thought patterns, goal orientation, and symbols orientation come from the subconscious. And we know that it is the other-than-conscious mind that deals with similes and metaphors, houses the imagination. We also know that the other-than-conscious mind deals best in terms of pictures and images. Brain researchers at The Center for the Mind at the University of Sydney tell us of the powerful problem-solving features of the subconscious mind:

> Striking accounts attest to the existence, and to the critical importance, of non-conscious problem solving...Essentially, a world of unconscious

17. L. Jancke (2000) *Cognitive Brain Research*, Vol. 10 (1–2), pp. 177–83.
18. Dennis R. Deaton (1996) *The Book on Mind Management*, MMI Publishing, p. 3.

information is sifted through, by mechanisms of which we are unaware, to arrive at our final judgments. For example, we have all experienced that the solution to a complex problem becomes apparent at a completely unexpected moment. The elusive key concept does not always appear when the problem is being actively pursued. Rather, it bizarrely appears unexpectedly when we are engaged in some completely unrelated task or thought process.[19]

Scientists continue to discover very startling things about the nature and power of the human mind. They tell us of the existence of the mind apart from the brain; the brain acting as the hardware by which the mind expresses itself. Some are even postulating the existence of a greater collective intelligence in the universe existing in what is referred to as the sub-manifest domain. This thinking coincides with what scientists have been telling us since the 1920s: the universe is not an empty void, but is filled with fields of energy. Elementary particles exist within relationships one with another and demonstrate synchronized actions even at a significant distance apart.

We know the mind is a powerful thing. Tapping into the full capability of the human brain is one of the keys to greater achievement and a cornerstone characteristic of our leadership model.

PURE KNOWLEDGE FUELS OUR ENGINE

The search for knowledge has been a noble and time-honored pursuit throughout the ages. Men and women from the beginning of time have been in search of answers to everything from the meaning of life to "who moved my cheese?". Our new leadership model is fueled by knowledge. Consider again the subconscious mind; problem-solving skills, ideation and creation, interpreting and assigning meaning all require data and information as fundamental fuel. But knowledge has to be more than simply an acquaintance with facts. It must include meaning, which can only be achieved through dialoging with others and through our experiences. I hardly need to ask which surgeon you would prefer for your heart bypass—a recent medical school graduate or the experienced physician.

We achieve meaning through experience—the practical application of theory. We learn from our experience by reflection and discussion of the experience—assigning our own meaning in terms of goals and expectations. Dialog gives us the opportunity to explore our informa-

19. Center for the Mind, University of Sydney, Sydney Australia, http://www.centreforthe-mind.com/research/researchers.htm, last accessed March 2002.

tion—to put it into a context and assign meaning. This interaction with others challenges our accepted wisdom and causes us to re-examine views, variables, and perceptions. Through this method, we are forced to pore over all positions, all theories, and all opinions in our search for the truth. Dialog is a process where there are no winners and losers, just winners: we win when we discover a truth, we win when we find a solution, and we win when we engage in collective thought.

A NEW VISION TAKING SHAPE

An improved personal leadership vision was beginning to take shape within me. I knew the vision must include creating a setting in which people could flourish, not just an atmosphere where the company could benefit. Our vision must embrace and recognize the value in understanding and harmonizing with the true nature of human beings, their relationship with each other, and with the universe of which we are all a part. This vision must make provision for the tapping of the more creative unconscious mind as well. It was time to view employees as more holistic, multi-faceted partners in the creation of enterprise. In my mind the old-style command-and-control management was dead forever.

So what do nature, the cosmos, and the untapped capabilities of people mean to our organizational vision? They mean that our vision must now embrace some of these doctrines:

1. The whole really is greater than the sum of the parts—nature is not a machine.
2. Human dialog is critical to creativity. When two ideas come together that never met before, they lead to or create a new idea.[20]
3. As we are all connected to the "cosmic database," it stands to reason that we must organize in a fashion that allows us to tap into this vast array of data.
4. Equilibrium is death to *The Quantum Organization*. If human interaction and dialog are critical fuel to the new organization, a little managed chaos thrown into our lives is essential to drive human creativity.
5. Complex systems such as organizations are best managed from the bottom up. Today's top-down, command-and-control management styles are complicated, inefficient, and problematic.
6. We must manage to recognize the tremendous individual human potential in the workplace. There must be a place at the corporate

20. For further discussion, see David Bohm (1996) *On Dialogue*, Routledge.

table for all employees, regardless of physical characteristics or role or position in the corporate hierarchy.

Our leadership vision is now beginning to take some genuine shape:

Our leadership mission is to create a setting in which human beings can flourish and are valued and recognized as the key to success. We will view employees as holistic, versatile partners in the creation of enterprise.

We will tap into the vast creative resources of the human mind in order to create our future. We will use pictures and sensory-rich descriptions of our goals to mine the immense capabilities of the subconscious mind.

We will engage in dialog with one another. We will recognize that we are all connected with nature, and we will learn to tap into that enormous cosmic database of knowledge. We will organize ourselves to take advantage of our connectedness. We will use self-forming teams to ensure that the best-qualified professionals are applied to the problems at hand.

We know that maintaining equilibrium in our lives and in enterprise stifles creativity. We will create a setting in which people are constantly in a state of transformation and where we are always stretching the creative capabilities of people. We will establish a set of fundamental principles for each of our complex systems. We will manage our systems by focusing on our fundamental principles or strange attractors.

I believe this mission statement, while probably not without its faults, gets at the core fundamentals of nature's true leadership qualities better than does our earlier version.

And now, finally, as we pry below the surface of the image of our leadership method, we are not disenchanted with our art. Rather, we are delighted at the beauty and the majesty of the finely tuned springs and mechanisms that we see when we put this new form into motion. And, out of the corner of our eye, briefly, we can imagine we glimpse the hand of God, the architect of it all.

It is now time to put what I had learned into practice.

Chapter 2

A Breakthrough:
Extending Human Creative Capability

NATURE and nature's laws lay hid in night; God said, "Let Newton be,"
and all was light. [1]

INTRODUCTION

Is it possible to create a work setting where people can truly thrive? And does it make sense to do so? We are not just talking about the well-being of the autocrat who lives at the top of the corporate food chain, we are talking about you and me—our co-workers—our friends.

Can we create such a place? Are we really able? WE CAN, WE ARE, AND WE WILL! We will not settle for anything less! We will create such a setting because when companies nuture their people—when they allow them to thrive—creativity and productivity soar. We are going to create such momentum, such obvious value, that we cannot be ignored; we cannot be stopped. We are going to demonstrate that the ill-advised corporate strategy of pandering to Wall Street instead of building true business value through people is simply wrong. This indiscriminate cut down of human resources is wrong today, and it will prove to be wide of the mark for tomorrow as well.

People really are a company's greatest asset, its most precious resource. It is up to us to prove it, to demonstrate the value of the individual through superior creativity leading to extraordinary output.

No industry is in need of such a paradigm shift more than the telecommunications industry. We have all been emotionally and economically crushed by:

1. Alexander Pope, epitaph intended for Sir Isaac Newton, in John Bartlett (1919) *Familiar Quotations.*

- The drop in business.
- The loss of jobs.
- The loss of corporate value.
- The slow-down in demand for telecommunications products and services.

Once the flagship industry in the national economy, telecommunications is now the poster-child for executive excesses, unrestrained and unsupported capital spending, and Wall Street overindulgences. The road back to the economic peak is going to be on the backs of middle managers like you. There are no more good ideas coming from the corporate *ivory* towers. Cutting away at corporate muscle is a vacant solution to the ills of the telecommunications industry. In fact, recent comprehensive studies show that after all the costs are examined, large indiscriminate downsizing really does nothing for the bottom line. Put simply, it just is not possible for companies to reduce their way to prosperity. Sorry, but we have been there and done that.

We will now explore some new methods and models that can identify and utilize the tremendous untapped human potential within all of us. We are entering the world of *The Quantum Organization.*

OUR CREATIVE SUBCONSCIOUS

The mind is a terrible thing to waste. We generally believe this to be true. Most often we relate it to the confused or misguided teen that fails to live up to his or her potential. But perhaps as big a tragic squander comes from our lack of understanding of the power of the subconscious mind.

Scientists tell us this about the other-than-conscious mind:

- The subconscious thinks in pictures and images.
- The subconscious never sleeps.
- The subconscious mind records everything it sees or hears.
- The subconscious can be given tasks.

In 1998, while working for a large telecommunications company in Denver, Colorado, I conducted some practical research on the capabilities of the subconscious mind. In fact, I put to the test all of the theories of *The Quantum Organization* that you will read about in this book. They are powerful, amazing, and somewhat startling—and most importantly they work.

One piece of research was conducted with two separate control groups—about 25 people. The objective was to test the following assertion:

> Using visual tools such as pictures and physical models in an ideation session will generate significantly more and better ideas and solutions to a problem than the more typical approach to brainstorming (i.e. going around the room and boarding ideas).

The research was conducted under the following conditions:

- The groups were both given the same problem and asked to board as many solutions as possible in 45 minutes.
- Each group had an independent observer to record the dynamics of the team interactions and group energy.
- The groups were sent to separate rooms to conduct the brainstorming
- Each team had similar make-up (i.e. human diversity).
- This research was conducted several times throughout a one-year period with different groups of people addressing different problems.

The results were amazing. In every case the team that used the physical models and pictures (the tools of the subconscious mind) generated significantly more solutions, had better team dynamics (better participation, more energy, more camaraderie), and had a better quality of solution than the traditional brainstorming teams.

In *The Quantum Organization* capturing the power of the other-than-conscious mind is central to our new leadership model. This is the wellspring of our new potential. This is where we will pull those groundbreaking creative new ideas that will drive real value for the corporation.

We will now discover how to harness this great asset we call the other-than-conscious mind.

THE POWER OF PICTURES AND IMAGES

We all know that the subconscious mind works in pictures and images. You know this from your own experiences. When was the last time you dreamed in paragraphs of text? So it stands to reason that pictures and images are the most effective way to communicate with the other-than-conscious mind.

The subconscious mind's workings are analogous to those of a computer. Requests and tasks are fed into the computer in a format that the machine understands. The tasks are processed until a solution is reached. Like the computer, the subconscious mind does not sleep, nor does it vary from its task until the problem is solved. There are two keys to harnessing the power of the other-than-conscious mind:

1. Feed the subconscious mind tasks to perform in the form of sensory-rich images and descriptions.
2. Recognize when the subconscious is giving you the answers you need.

To get online with the other-than-conscious mind, we can do the following:

- Create one-page documents that through pictures, images, and descriptive text pose questions—problems to be solved.
- Review these descriptive queries on a regular basis—at least once daily.
- Set aside time to ponder and allow the subconscious to work on the problem(s).
- Sleep on it.
- Be receptive to those flashes of learning, the sudden intuitive perception or insight in the essential meaning of something.
- Record what you have learned, what the subconscious is telling you, and begin working on your action plans.
- Use this process over and over again.

I assure you this process works—it works for any problem, whether it is that new product idea, or as you struggle to develop or repair a personal relationship. This powerful and knowledgeable personal computer that you have at your fingertips can be your most valued asset—the key to the power to create your future.

One final and very important thought—feed your mind. Feed your *personal computer* with what it craves—data. In other words, READ! Read the best authors, read the newspaper, magazines, and newsletters —read them all. Never let a day go by when you are not empowering your subconscious mind with the muscle it needs to work for you.

THE INFLUENCE OF LANGUAGE

We have talked somewhat about the power of pictures and images, particularly as they relate to the subconscious mind. As you put the ideology that you are learning in this book into practice, the power of language will be critical to your successful implementation of the principles of *The Quantum Organization*. We are now going to explore the amazing power of language—of words and the thoughts they represent.

What pictures and images come to your mind when you see or hear the words "Just Do It"? These are three simple and common words used in everyday conversation, yet they conjure up a most commanding emotional response in most of the literate world. A key to integrating your message, or your mission, throughout your organization is the creation of new language, new words that evoke the same kind of emotional response as the Nike theme. You do not have to invent new words, but you must create, from the words that you know, new phrases that can be linked to the images and ideas you create—that can be linked to your new leadership paradigm.

CONFIDENCE OF CONVICTION

In this book we have been, and will yet be, introduced to many new and exciting principles of *The Quantum Organization*. Many go counter to what we have been taught all of our lives. Faith is a principle of action. It is by our belief that a principle is true that we are compelled to act, to go about the business of accomplishment enthusiastically. In other words, through our thoughts and actions we can create the world we want to live in. As you read this book, I ask you to listen to the still-small voice, your intuition, to know if these principles are true. You will know the verity of these things as you feel a sense of calm assurance. You will be synchronized with the powers of nature; and by this power, you can know the truth of all things.

Finally, as an undeviating tribute to *you*—the individual, the true engine of change—the enduring words of Helen Keller, "Life is either a daring adventure or nothing at all."

Chapter 3

A Quantum Leap:
Stunning New Leadership Tools

*HOW wonderful that we have met with a paradox. Now we have some
hope of making progress.*[1]

INTRODUCTION

On many a warm summer day in Colorado, after a vigorous bicycle
ride through the cottonwood trees and meadows of Douglas
County, I often find myself resting among the wildflowers along
Cherry Creek. It is a quiet, restful place. The stream wanders to the
contours of the land and flows effortlessly under the bridge beside my
hidden place.

For months I have been watching a neighborhood of Barn
Swallows, birds we sometimes call Mud Daubers, building their homes
beneath the planks and beams of the bridge. Their supplies are the mud
and sticks; the slivers and fragments they harvest along the periphery
of the stream. They work as an integrated unit. They seem to me
almost as a single organism, single in purpose yet with agency and
individualism. I have an impression of their sense of cooperation and
community—their connectedness. There is no chief snapping out
orders, no project lieutenant insuring that each stick and daub of mud
is placed according to policy. There are no meetings, no e-mails, no
memos, no commands, yet the birds work in unison with singleness of
purpose and well-ordered accomplishment.

I have often thought of this scene and contemplated how this form
might be applied in the workplace. Could we really have such unison
and singleness of purpose, that same connectedness that I observed in
the birds? The answer is yes we can—we call it *The Quantum
Organization.*

1. Quotations from Niels Bohr,
    http://www-gap.dcs.st and.ac.uk/history/Quotations/Bohr_Niels

Let us examine some very specific techniques for building *The Quantum Organization*, including management tools and processes that you can start using today.

WHAT IS IN OUR QUANTUM TOOL KIT?

As a prelude to submerging ourselves into techniques we used to pull together our *Quantum Organization*, I want to tell you a little bit about our team, our purpose, and our objectives. We were a group of about twenty marketing, training, financial, and forecasting professionals. Our group's responsibilities were to build business strategies for the wholesale division of a large telecommunications carrier headquartered in Denver, Colorado. Our customers were the myriad emerging competitive providers of telecom services that would ultimately contend with the retail arm of the firm.

It was our task to pull together the strategies and programs that would make the wholesale division successful, and more than just a moneymaking and growing concern. We had a responsibility to fuel the rising competitive machinery, to enable the up-and-coming companies that would vie for a piece of the telecommunications pie. Our friends on our retail side of the business were not always so happy with us, and in fact they were quite a formidable roadblock to our success much of the time.

As a team, after significant reflection and study, it was our aim to do something different, something out of the ordinary and perhaps even outrageous. We needed a stratagem that would drive real change and long-term value for the company and for the people. Our line of attack had to be enduring and we hoped, and perhaps we even knew, that it would jar traditional thinking. It would take a quantum leap in thinking, a change in the accepted wisdom. We needed a new vision and visionary conduct to follow.

What follows is a synopsis of our work, our attempt at unfettered creativity, backed up by science, and a discussion of some of the tools we used to help us breathe life into our *Quantum Organization*.

DIALOG/EXPLORATION

Dialog, or the exploration of ideas through dialog, is a foundational characteristic of *The Quantum Organization*. To best describe dialog let me tell you what dialog is not. Dialog is not debate—debate kills creativity. In a debate there are two sides and one eventual winner. With dialog (in meetings and amongst ourselves) we create an exchange of those ideas with the purpose of creating a third (improved) solution. Our dialog sessions were our most treasured moments. We so enjoyed the exchange of ideas and the free-spirited and energized ideation that took place. We really looked forward to these meetings. We had four inviolate rules for dialog:

1. No criticism of another's ideas is allowed.
2. There are to be no winners and losers; simply put, there is to be no debate—when anybody wins, we all win.
3. Each and every team member must participate—it is the duty of each participant to make sure everyone has a chance to contribute.
4. We never leave an idea or a topic unless we are all ready to move on—in dialog there are no agendas.

As I look back over our experience and experimentation with dialog no single event or moment stands out in my mind. It is more the process of dialog and the many small, yet meaningful connections that were made one with another. This is not to say that there were not some mighty and memorable moments during our dialog sessions. Several new ideas were proffered that led to new products and new product features, there were new business directions set and clarifications of existing strategies realized, and we had more than a few potent flashes of brilliance and blazes of tremendous personal growth.

The renowned physicist and great thinker David Bohm says this about dialog:

> The object of a dialog is not to analyze things, or to win an argument, or to exchange opinions. Rather, it is to suspend your opinions and to look at the opinions—to listen to everybody's opinions, to suspend them, and to see what all that means. If we can see what all of our opinions mean, then we are sharing a common content...I think that when we are able to sustain a dialog of this sort you will find that there will be a change in the people taking part.[2]

Over time we began to know each other quite well and in terms of our relationships, the more time we spent together in dialog the closer we became. We were able to get into a cogent and meaningful dialog very rapidly. We could easily share our thoughts and it was as if we were able to think together—to focus collectively our minds as we discussed the topics of the moment. We would begin our dialog without a leader and without an agenda. This was not a time for pop-up leadership—

2. David Bohm (1996) *On Dialogue*, Routledge, p. 26.

this was a time for equal freethinkers to come together to explore new ideas without constraints.

ORGANIZATIONAL CONFIGURATIONS

It stands to reason that many organizational configurations can and must make sense in fluid *networks* like *Quantum Organization*s. We offer one such example below (self-forming teams). Having said that, here are some characteristics that every configuration might have:

- Relationships within the networks are the key.
- These are learning organizations adaptable to change.
- Ideas are allowed to come forth not by force or hierarchical power, but because they make sense.
- No person or group is independent from the others.
- We have richness as a result of diversity of view and experience.
- The organizational focus is not a matter of who will solve the problem but what wisdom and skill is brought to the table to solve it.
- The old paradigm declares the only way to motivate people is to push them and to prod them; we now know that motivation comes from unrestricted freedom.

SELF-FORMING TEAMS

Self-forming teams come into being as need arises to support the work that must get done. We no longer think of people and their roles in the organization as fixed and permanent structures. Creating *The Quantum Organization* is a process of building and applying relationships and not one of a specific hierarchy. Joseph Jaworski in his book *Synchronicity* makes very clear the interconnectedness of nature and human beings. Following on the principles of synchronicity, the notion of self-forming teams brings people together, the people with the appropriate skills, in a very dynamic and synchronous fashion to solve problems and get work done.

In the Fall of 2000 a most spectacular discovery was made regarding dynamic organizational structure or self-forming teams. We sometimes referred to these self-defining structures as pop-up organizations. I had been doing some extensive research in self-organizing structures and felt it was time to put some of the concepts into practice. I was interested in creating a group with the following characteristics:

1. Focus on problem solving.
2. Dynamic make-up in terms of team members.
3. Empowered pop-up leadership—leader for one project and a follower for the next.
4. Independence of my participation or input.
5. Use of creative tools to generate ideas.

It was believed that the following benefits would be derived from self-forming structures:

- Ability to apply the best resource to a problem rapidly.
- Creation of organizational structures that could make fast decisions.
- Provision of leadership opportunities and experience to a broader segment of the employee body.
- Improvement (as measured by speed and quality) of internal communication.

There were three challenges ahead of me that were mine to address:

1. The team needed training—some formal classroom instruction on the concept of self-forming teams.
2. They also needed some sort of catalyst or example of a self-forming team in action to give them the case example that they would draw upon as they developed their own pop-up structures.
3. I needed to have patience and allow the team to form as well as the resolve to stay out of the process and let it mature without upper-management meddling.

At the time I was not sure I could do number three so I started with the training and hoped for the best. I put together several dialog-based training seminars and invited the entire management team to attend. As a team we held several of these sessions and worked out the concepts together. We talked about temporary and dynamic leadership, and we discussed forming support teams based on the nature of the issue—based on needs. We explored the difficulties of prioritizing and scheduling under such fluid circumstances; we talked about the importance of building and maintaining relationships throughout the life of the project, we worked on breaking down the old paradigm of hierarchical reporting and performance reviews, and much more.

We determined that in order for the training to work each of the members of the team had to exhibit some or all of the following qualities:

- *Courage*: to step up and take the lead in the absence of a leader.
- *Humility*: to sometimes allow the pigeons to lead the eagles.
- *Ownership*: to recognize a need and stick with it until it is met.
- *Diversity*: to insure that the best resources are brought to bear.
- *Creativity*: to get to the best solution.
- *Service*: to remember that people truly are our greatest asset.

With the training complete and the team fired-up and ready to go, I needed a catalyst—some sort of case example to kick-off this experiment. An opportunity presented itself about two weeks after the training was completed. I wish I could say that I pre-planned everything that happened, but frankly I seized upon an opportunity and let it play out.

Our leadership team was again assembled for a weekly strategy development meeting. In this gathering a typical agenda would include plan development, issues, questions and answers, and reviewing action items. This particular day we were poised to address the communications plan; this was the plan to share the corporate strategy with the mass of employees in the Division. I was the Chair of the meeting so it was up to me to kick things off and go about the business of meeting the agenda. On this day, I decided today we would do things a little bit differently. Instead of kicking off the meeting I sat at the head of the table as usual but said nothing—absolutely nothing. A couple of silent minutes went by—five minutes turned into ten—ten into twenty. By this time the uneasiness of the group was obvious. There were nervous snickers and some jostling around in seats, but still I said nothing. Someone asked me if we were waiting for someone, but still I said nothing.

This went on for some time until finally it dawned on one of the team what was going on. After a few more unanswered questions the group finally understood the exercise and as if by magic the energy in the room was palpable. Over the course of the next hour leaders emerged, ideas were generated, plans made and readied for execution. I was now convinced of the power and value of self-forming structures—I had seen it with my own eyes.

Over the course of the next several months there were other opportunities to watch these pop-up teams in action—it was clear that they worked[3] and that the results from these teams were superior. It was

3. As measured by:
- Better quality decisions—less mistakes and rework.
- Decisions were being made closer to the problem.
- Additional opportunities for team members to be put in positions of leadership—to gain experience.
- Better team morale and a broader sharing of key data and information.

also evident that when working under these conditions there was a harmony or synchronicity between the people—we knew that this was the way nature intended us to interrelate.

INFORMATION HUB

The information hub has both an informal and a formal nature. The informal component can be the exchanges of thoughts and ideas around the water cooler, or the discussions during dialog or those taking place over lunch. The more formal part takes on the look and feel of a board or commission. This commission is responsible for ensuring that information is collected and stored and is content rich, up to date, and available to all. It also serves as a forum for discussion of issues, work to be done, priorities, and what teams will come together to work on problems.

In our first attempt at information hubs we learned a lot through experience—through trial and error. We started by building a central team, a group of aggressive learners that loved to read and discover new things. We charged this group with collecting and filtering data and information. As all of us know, there is no shortage of information. The World Wide Web has insured us of a constant flow of huge amounts of data. The trick is to find ways to catalog the data for timely retrieval and to filter out the good information from the bad. Two of our early challenges were:

1. Establishing a functioning and integrated Information Hub while continuing to meet the demands of the business. In other words, the Information Hub is key to the success of our new organization. Getting the hub in place and functioning with a rich collection of data takes time.
2. Providing a process or mechanism to make the data readily available to any and all that desire access.

Confronting the issues surrounding item one above was daunting. We tried to start small—bringing only a limited collection of data online. The problem was obvious: without a rich catalog of data we were limited in our opportunities to apply it. Waiting until the hub is fully functional and loaded with a comprehensive set of information takes too much time. We knew that the new organization structure plays a key role in defining and assigning work—the hub needs to be online immediately and we would just have to wait for the data. We struggled with somewhat disorganized data catalogs and holes in our data for a time. But each day was better than the one before and eventually we had a functional and effective hub that was integrated into the organization and helping to deliver creative solutions.

Item two was a bit simpler–there was an effective technology solution right before our eyes–the web. With the help of an outside contractor, we built a very powerful web-based tool that we called the Quick Reference Guide (QRG). The QRG provided easy access and an understandable organization for all of our data; it provided tips and best practices, and it provided a great repository for training materials. The information hub is a vital catalyst for focused learning and a means for the building of knowledge and wisdom in the organization.

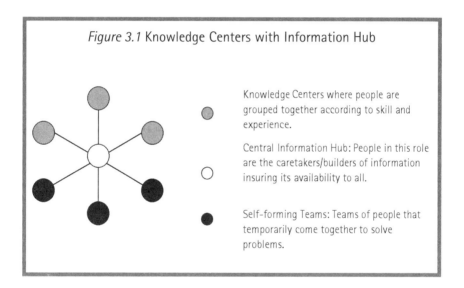

Figure 3.1 Knowledge Centers with Information Hub

Knowledge Centers where people are grouped together according to skill and experience.

Central Information Hub: People in this role are the caretakers/builders of information insuring its availability to all.

Self-forming Teams: Teams of people that temporarily come together to solve problems.

Finally, knowledge–the attainment and application of information–is one of the three key principles of *The Quantum Organization*. Information hubs help teams to store, organize, and retrieve information. The defining characteristic of an information hub is the notion that people and the vast amounts of information stored in our brains are part of this central repository of information–the untapped wellspring of knowledge. Information hubs are not defined as electronic databases filled with bits and bytes–ones and zeroes. They are not file cabinets bloated with manila folders and scores of documents. An information hub certainly can include all of these things, but it is much more. It includes a catalog of information and knowledge regardless of where it might reside–the database, the file cabinet–and most importantly the human mind.

MODELS AS A CREATIVE TOOL

One of the most remarkable and beneficial techniques in our tool-kit is that of the visual model. We literally (using crayons, styrofoam, glitter, and glue) built physical models to help us see through the old systems that constrain us. Todd Siler, in his book *Think Like A Genius*,[4] calls these models *Metaphorms*. Metaphorming is a process of connecting two or more otherwise unrelated ideas, examining any commonalities, exploring these commonalities by drawing pictures or building models of the ideas together, and then analyzing, through dialog, what you have developed in terms of new ideas, thoughts, and revelations.

At an executive leadership meeting held in Phoenix, Arizona in late 1999, we had the opportunity to again put modeling to the test. For one of the business development breakout sessions we had a unique opportunity for some additional research. The audience was divided into six separate groups. All of the groups were given the same business problem to solve but each group was to use a different facilitation method to arrive at their solution. All of the teams had the same allotted time (60 minutes) and were monitored by trained facilitators.

Group 1 (*The Brainstormers*) was placed in a conference room and instructed to use the traditional brainstorming methodology of going around the room suggesting ideas and listing them on paper. The session ended when the group had listed every possible solution they could think of.

Group 2 (*The Mixers*) was given several predetermined solutions and they played a match game of sorts; they mixed and matched solutions against subsets of the problem. This method is used to stimulate creative thinking as the team discussed the potential results of the various combinations of solutions.

Group 3 (*The Debaters*) was sent to a conference room where a traditional debate took place between supporters of two different solutions to the problem. The group formed two teams and the debate began. The purpose of this exercise was to see if the group using the somewhat confrontational technique of debate could emerge with additional and perhaps better solutions to the business problem.

Groups 4, 5, and 6 (*The Modelers*) were given kits consisting of styrofoam shapes, pipe cleaners, magazine pictures, glitter, glue, markers, wooden dowels, and a whole collection of other arts and crafts

4. Todd Siler (1997) *Think Like A Genius*, Bantam Books.

materials. They were asked to create visual models of their solution. The teams were given a short list of instructions regarding the process of modeling:

1. Everyone works on the model simultaneously.
2. Open interactive discussion is encouraged.
3. Use the crafts kits to build an image (metaphor) of the solution(s).

As the facilitators monitored progress they were able to observe the unique dynamics of each group.

The Brainstormers

The facilitators commented that this group looked tense and worn out towards the end of the session. This group was dominated by two strong personalities who led the bulk of the discussion. The first few minutes yielded some new ideas and exhibited a high level of energy. This energy was evident as long as the ideas were flowing—once the idea generation dwindled, so did the excitement and the discussion. After about fifteen minutes the group felt they had exhausted their ideas and went on to discuss irrelevant topics. Several members indicated privately that they felt intimidated by senior managers and were inhibited from offering critical input for fear of reprisal.

The Mixers

This group exhibited a high level of energy and it was obvious that the members of this team were engaged in the process and having fun. One dominant personality emerged to the lead the team and the discussion. The random mixing and matching of predetermined solutions to problems created some "out of the box" thinking and generated several additional non-traditional solutions. However, this group was also dominated by strong personalities that tended to monopolize the discussion.

The Debaters

While this group exhibited energy and spirit, the adversarial nature of the debate format led to no generation of new ideas. Creativity and non-traditional thinking were glaringly absent in this group. In a few cases individuals tried to breakout of the process and interject some new thinking and new ideas, but other members of the group quickly herded them back in the fold.

The Modelers

Back in the main conference area it looked like a class of kindergarten kids had invaded the room. The conversation was deafening—people were laughing and having fun without regard to personality or rank. Everyone was covered in glitter—some even had it in their teeth! The volume of ideas, thoughts, and strategies that emerged from this process was of greater magnitude than any of the other teams. There was no opportunity for dominant personalities to overshadow the more meek and mild of the group; this process does not require an individual leader to come forward and take over.

Here in a ballroom of a grand hotel were mature adults playing with pipe cleaners, glue, and glitter, learning how to be creative again. They were applying simple tools to generate complex solutions for multifaceted business problems. The dialog was almost raucous and middle managers through senior management were working and playing side by side. When the allotted time expired, the modelers refused to stop—they were still generating and discussing additional solutions—the energy in the room was growing stronger by the minute.

The real benefits from the modeling process came with the examining of the models and exploring, through dialog, the different perceptions of what the model represented. We gained the greatest advantage when team members let their minds go, when they were able to see past the existing paradigms that limit one's view.

DISEQUILIBRIUM

Putting forth ideas, thoughts, principles, and paradoxes is important to creating the instability in the system responsible for initiating change. This is the practice of disequilibrium: introducing new relationships and information that pricks our thinking and challenges the collective wisdom. It is the role of disequilibrium to jar the organization. It is this disruption that causes us to examine more variables, to engage the creative machinery—to continually self-evaluate.

One event that helps us to illustrate the principle of disequilibrium occurred on 9 May 1988. A fire wiped out an Illinois Bell central office in Hinsdale, Illinois. The Hinsdale fire occurred on Mother's Day, one of the busiest calling days of the year. The fire started deep within a cable trough and smoldered in the unattended building for some time before tripping the fire alarms. It destroyed the building and disrupted service to many throughout the Chicago area.

It is not so much the fire itself or the lengthy telephone outage that we are interested in. We are attracted to the all but miraculous restoration of phone service that occurred. In this fire over 38,000 customers were affected; there were 9,000 businesses with over 100,000 employees impacted. The service was restored by 20 May—eleven days later. Normal everyday experience with your phone company may be different from mine, but it has taken more than eleven days on occasion to get a single telephone line installed to my home—let alone 38,000. You probably know that it takes many months and sometimes years to get major pieces of telephone switching equipment built and delivered. This is not the kind of gear that is sitting on the shelf at your local Circuit City. Some of this gear is custom built and only upon demand.

The restoration of this telephone office is considered by some in the industry as the greatest single disaster recovery in the history of telecommunications. In this recovery creativity ruled—processes and forms were put aside, and free agency of the individual was evident. I would not suggest interjecting this kind of pandemonium into your business, but it demonstrates how we rise to the occasion with a little disequilibrium. We put on our thinking caps—when we have to get creative, we do. The greatest destructive force in terms of our creativity is equilibrium—the ruts we create for ourselves in the name of Office Practice, Total Quality Management, or Kaizen.

QUANTUM LANGUAGE

The Quantum Organization demands its own language, the words and phrases that immediately call to mind the character of the system; the pictures and images of the new world we are creating. It is through new language of this nature that we can engage the minds of the people—to open their eyes to the relationships that are so important to our success—to communicate meaning. A few examples of would-be language of *The Quantum Organization* follow:

- *Disequilibrium*: the interjection of new information and relationships that challenge the organization; causes the system to constantly reevaluate itself.
- *Self-organizing*: organizations that evolve and change dynamically to address the needs of the system.
- *Learning Organizations*: recognition that information is ever changing, and that the organization must evolve with the information.
- *Participative World*: vibrancy of order and accomplishment is a direct result of the numbers and kinds of people who participate in the learning and the doing.

- *Organizational Intelligence*: recognizing that it is the collective wisdom of the team, not any one person, that brings success and accomplishment.
- *Strange Attractor*: the few controlling core components of a complex system.
- *Mind Management*: understanding the full potential of the human mind and then applying it to our life.
- *Quantum Organization*: the collection of scientific, creative, and intellectual principles that form the foundation of a new leadership paradigm.
- *Pure Knowledge*: the search for all truth and the combination of those truths and our experiences.
- *Dialog*: the act of sharing ideas in a non-confrontational format that encourages discussion of all opinions in order to establish a common content.

I am not suggesting that new words or acronyms be created—the words we have available to us are sufficient. This is about creating meaning and assigning that meaning to words and phrases. We can paint some very vivid pictures and images in the minds of our stakeholders and we can call these images to mind through our language.

STRANGE ATTRACTORS

A very powerful quantum instrument is referred to in complexity science as strange attractor. "Strange attractors" are the few controlling core components of a complex system such as an organization. If you can find the three or four fundamental driving principles of a system and focus attention on them, the rest of the structure will take care of itself. By way of example, let us examine a tree: trying to manage the health and well-being of every leaf and branch individually would be a hopeless exercise in ineffectiveness. However, if you attend to the roots of the tree, the leaves and branches will emerge with form and beauty.

Some fundamental principles, or strange attractors, in a business management setting might be: set the vision and mission, change the language, establish the leadership theory, and communicate the strategy (see Figure 3.2).

If a leader would spend his or her time focusing on these four components of the business, complexity theory (and our experience) says the details of the enterprise would unfold with richness, order, and accomplishment.

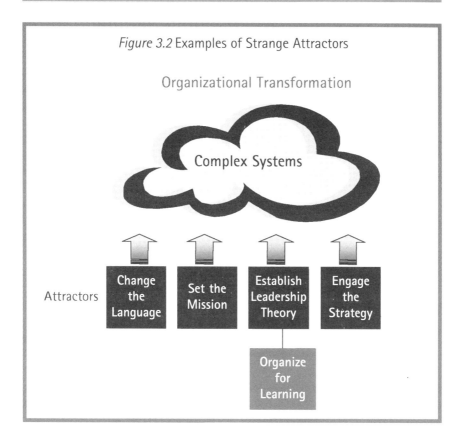

Figure 3.2 Examples of Strange Attractors

In 1998 we began an organizational transformation—we started down a path to redefine our business. A commitment was made by the senior leader to transform the company from a reactive and sluggish monopoly to a nimble and proactive competitor. In order to do this we needed a total redesign of almost every process in the division. We needed a forward-looking business strategy, a comprehensive market and customer information database, a rapid product development process, a new learning/training model, and new leadership with the vision to bring this new paradigm to life.

We set out to build the plan. We started by constructing a planning process that touched all aspects of the business. It addressed our need for data, and a lot of it. We collected business drivers, indicators that lead and lag the market; we redefined the value chain and our value proposition.

We collected mountains of data and business intelligence about our industry, the market, and our competition. We painted a very detailed view of our customers, our competitors, and our customers' needs and

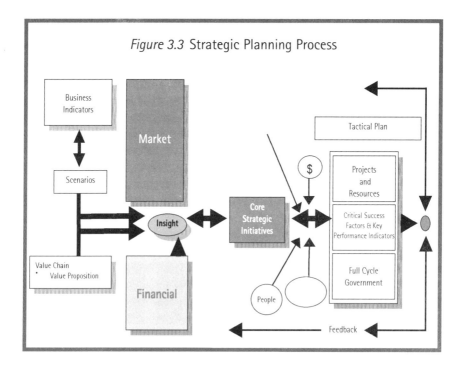

Figure 3.3 Strategic Planning Process

desires. On top of this we collected financial data and created product and service forecasts.

All of this data came together with the best minds we could muster for analysis—we called this our insight sessions. We worked for days upon days analyzing data and formulating the core strategies that would guide our company to financial success—we had a strategy from which we established our vision and mission for the company, and we had our attractors:

1. Set the vision.
2. Change the language.
3. Establish leadership theory and learning strategy.
4. Engage the strategy.

To communicate this strategy and change the organization we set about developing new strategic vision for the company. We built a powerful multi-media communications message that we delivered to each employee in the division. In our message we created language with new meaning; we talked about developing products in Internet time, we introduced the notion of Value Innovation, talked about share-of-customer vs market share, and carved out a new way to deal with government regulators. We also introduced the concept of *Quantum Organizations* and went about training the executive leadership teams in these new principles.

This was not a one-time event—this process defined our work for the months and years to come. As a strategy team, we dedicated every working moment to the four attractors (Fab Four) we defined. We spent no time worrying about how the Product people built products and likewise we spent no effort hounding Sales to insure that the message given to customers was in lockstep with the strategic plan. We knew that if we spent our time on the Fab Four the rest of the organization would emerge with form and beauty—and it did.

VISUAL REAL-TIME FEEDBACK

In the spring of 2000 we conducted a very revealing experiment regarding a concept that I call *Visual Real-time Feedback (VRF)*. The Wholesale Strategy Team developed this technique to help us determine if the strategies we were developing for the division were 1) being comprehended, and 2) accepted or, in other words, if there was general agreement amongst our constituents and stakeholders for the strategic direction we were setting.

Let me describe the setting in which this experiment took place. We were gathered together in an offsite location in a huge room normally used for training large groups. At the head of the room was a small stage with raised podium and microphone, slide projector, and projection screen. The tables and chairs in the body of the room were arrayed in a horseshoe configuration in order to insure that everyone in the room could easily see both the podium and the other attendees. This was a board meeting of the stakeholders of the 2000 Wholesale Division Strategic Plan. The main purpose of this meeting was to deliver detailed descriptions of several new strategic concepts and get consensus from the group to move forward and begin execution of the plan.

Using masking tape and other arts and crafts materials we created a large matrix on the floor of the room similar to the one pictured in Figure 3.4.

This exercise was absolutely priceless in its ability to allow speaker interaction with a small- to medium-sized audience, to get clear and immediate feedback regarding the clarity of communication, and to understand in real-time the degree to which the audience agrees or disagrees with your message.

Figure 3.4 Visual Real-time Feedback

Don't Understand Agree	Understand Agree
Don't Understand Don't Agree	Understand Don't Agree

This is how it works:

1. The audience participants are asked to stand in the square labeled "Don't Understand - Don't Agree" at the beginning of each presentation.
2. The speaker is asked to step up onto the stage and prepare to deliver his or her presentation from the raised podium. The elevated nature of the stage allows the presenter to see the matrix on the floor clearly and each of the audience participants.
3. The audience participants are instructed to move freely about within the matrix during the presentation and stand according to how well they understand the speaker's message and to what degree they agree with it.
4. The speaker is free to stop the presentation at any point and inquire of the audience the thinking and reasoning behind their choice of location on the matrix.

Throughout the presentation the locations of the audience in the matrix change according to how well the speaker clarifies his or her concepts and to what degree the listener agrees with the message, as depicted in Figure 3.5.

We found that after the presenter got comfortable with the distractions of the rustle of movement, he or she was energized by the interactivity with the audience and the dynamic character of the presentation that was otherwise designed to be a somewhat typical (dull) one-way communication. Real-time dialog created a tremendous

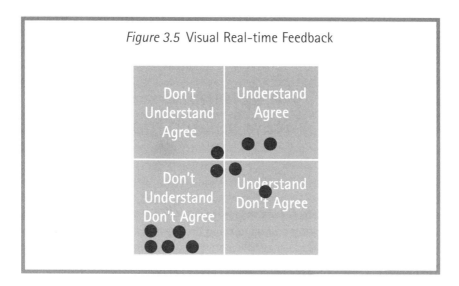

Figure 3.5 Visual Real-time Feedback

learning experience for both the audience and the presenter. New ideas and concepts were generated and new disciples of the quantum were converted. We also discovered a small side benefit: this is a great tool to allow the speaker to interact with a test group to anticipate questions and to prepare and refine his or her delivery to an actual audience.

All of the techniques[5] described in this chapter are the product of years of scientific research and countless experiments and trials by error. Each of the tools works—they are all in harmony with the scientific theories that underpin them and they have been shown to be effective in actual practice.

5. Dialog, see David Bohm (1996) *On Dialogue*, Routledge; Visual vs test see Dennis R. Deaton (1996) *The Book on Mind Management*; Self-forming Teams see Joseph Jaworski (1996) *Synchronicity*, Berrett-Koehler; Strange Attractors see Roger Lewin (1999) *Complexity*, University of Chicago Press; Metaphorming see Todd Siler (1997) *Think Like A Genius*, Bantam Books; Synchronizing with Nature see Deepak Chopra (2000) *The Conscious Universe*, Hay House Audio.

Chapter 4

An Epiphany:
Building a New Leadership Model

THAT is just the way with some people. They get down on a thing when they don't know nothing about it. [1]

INTRODUCTION

We were all in the room for what appeared to the casual observer to be yet another of a countless number of corporate meetings. We were meeting as the Strategy Leadership Team and around the table were the brain trust; the best and the brightest and the most diverse we could muster. We loved these gatherings: they were exhilarating, electrifying, and filled with vitality. No one knew quite what to expect at the finish; no one knew what leaps we would take or what transformations would occur. We were in great harmony one with another; at peace with ourselves and with the business in which we were engaged.

Our experiment into *The Quantum Organization* was in its infancy— just beginning to take some shape. Nevertheless, already we knew that the principles and doctrines of *The Quantum Organization* were real and true. We knew that we could never willingly go back to the way we were; we could never freely follow a leader or work for a company that was not in harmony with these principles. Of course, we knew that we would not always be able to choose with whom we worked, but we were committed to revolutionize the workplace wherever or with whomever our paths intersected.

BUILDING AN ADVANTAGE THROUGH HARMONY

The process of synchronizing with nature means understanding our

1. Mark Twain (1912) *The Adventures of Huckleberry Finn*, Harper & Brothers, p. 3.

true nature as defined by quantum physics, and organizing and managing people according to those principles created great harmony within the workgroup and great confidence within the individual. We had a fluid motion within the team, an affinity with efficiency; we emerged an integrated squad. Another byproduct was an enormous ability to focus, to continue the learning. We were drinking up everything we could on the topic of the quantum, self-esteem building, the nature of the universe, the value of the individual, and the connectedness that we all felt.

One of the most profound moments, and as it turned out the cornerstone of our learning, came during a modeling (Metaphorming) session with the entire team. In Metaphorming, the first task that must be completed is to agree upon a question to be answered or an issue to be tackled. In this opening session we began with the question, "Who am I and as a person what is important to me?" In other words, what are my values, my abilities, desires, likes, and dislikes?

Each of us began to build a physical model of who we were, our value system, our priorities, our loves, and passions. We spent about 90 of the most creative and revealing minutes of our lives building and then communicating to each other and ourselves our innermost thoughts and beliefs. This session was designed to accomplish the following:

1. Reveal as much about personal priorities as possible.
2. Capture the true diverse nature of the group and build appreciation for that diversity.
3. Allow the team to bond.
4. Uncover personal- and management-style techniques that help or hinder teambuilding.
5. Help people get in touch with who they are and how they come across to others.

One of the attendees was having some difficulty with her team members. Ruth spoke of the relationship with her team as being distant and sometimes confrontational. Her diverse group consisted of people with varying degrees of education, cultural backgrounds, management styles, personalities, and genders. Ruth was a dedicated manager who spent many of her evenings in the office completing high-profile projects assigned to her department. Her only complaint was that she often needed to work late in order to insure that the work was done right— sometimes the only way to get it right is to do it yourself she often said. Ruth attended our session hoping to discover why her workgroup would not respond to her management style or bond as a team.

As the attendees began to create their models, Ruth was busy cutting out pictures from publications and stacking them into very neat piles. It was well into the session when Ruth began to assemble her pieces. She began to construct a box structure that resembled the walls of a house, with a roof-like arrangement on the top. At one of the corners was a small gap that allowed some visibility into the structure. The outside of the house was a patchwork of highly energetic imagery of fast cars, ski resorts, fashion models, sports figures, along with more urbane images of college campuses and business settings.

After the models were finished, we moved to Phase 2 of the session where each person gives an oral readout of their model and responds to questions from the group. As Ruth described her model, she stayed very focused on the exterior walls and you could sense her enthusiasm about the physical activities in which she was involved.

Through the gap in the corner, you could peer inside her structure and there you saw a very different interior. The inside contained pictures of families, children, and spiritual images that seemed in contrast to the outside. As Ruth elaborated on each representation on the inside, she became more emotional almost to the point of tears. For Ruth, this was a moment that she probably feared. In her world, showing emotion in the workplace is not acceptable—especially in front of her colleagues. The group encouraged her to continue sharing her most personal experiences—it was difficult, yet powerful and revealing.

She explained the importance she placed on being accepted by people including the group she managed. Ruth went on to share that her mother demanded nothing less than perfection from her during her youth and perhaps that explained her inability to trust others with important work.

It was the group's turn to provide feedback to Ruth regarding what they noticed in her model and how she was perceived in the workplace. The group described her house in literal terms and confirmed that the Ruth they knew looked just like the images on the outside of her model. We went on to further share with her that the walls she put up prevented anyone from getting to know the real Ruth. And it was with the whole person that the group was just now connecting. Someone noted that to connect with those around us, we must move past the exterior facade and get to know the whole person before we can achieve true diversity and celebrate our differences.

Each member of the group took their turn reading out their model and participating in the feedback session. This was the most powerful and moving workshop I have ever experienced in the workplace. The participants came away from this activity changed forever. We had laid the foundation for deep and lasting relationships—relationships that are strong to this day. New and significant skills, capabilities, and interests were uncovered that were immediately applicable to current projects—we started new projects based on what we learned that day. Perhaps the most valuable thing we learned was how to serve one another—how we could help each other to learn and grow. We created a bond within the team that cannot be broken and was foundational to establishing team trust and trustworthiness.

CHANGING HOW WE TRUST

The key to making *The Quantum Organization* actually happen is creating an atmosphere of trust. To encourage and convince people to take risks can only happen when trust is part of the foundation. This means strong relationships, as we will discuss later. It entails friendship and caring; it implies community. It gives rise to physically powerful bonds between people. Trust is really foundational to healthy associations on the job as well as in all walks of life.

What we found to our surprise and mortification was how little real trust existed in our workplace. We uncovered a foundational flaw in our workplace relationships. We were surprised because we felt like our group was exceptionally close and well adjusted. We were mortified because of the huge gulf that we had discovered between us and who we thought we were and who we wanted to be. We saw the chinks in our armor of self-image.

We had to close the gap of our fear and suspicion sufficiently to allow *The Quantum Organization* to form. There was no shortcut to closing this gulf. There was no silver bullet; there was no quick fix. Foundations of trust take time to pour and a lifetime to cure. Our key to establishing trust was to be trustworthy. We each had to take ownership of the problem of trustworthiness. We had to take risks, we had to allow failure, and we had to be willing to forgive and to learn from our mistakes. We started by revealing personal information about ourselves and we trusted the team to be discreet with that delicate information.

CREATING SELF-ASSURED FREE THINKERS

Another powerful improvement that emerged from the team was the rise in individual confidence, which in turn resulted in self-assured freethinkers. We were all amazed at the increase in the self-confidence of the individual as we were able to express our otherwise submerged thoughts and ideas. We had no fears of negative criticism when new or off-the-wall opinions were presented for discussion within the group.

We had been successful in changing the culture from one of suspicion and selfishness to one of compassion, hungry for new ideas and thoughts, regardless of how well that notion was developed. We allowed, and even demanded, that diverse beliefs and views were raised before the group and then developed. Each of us had a great sense of accomplishment, as our partially developed ideas were built-up and successfully implemented.

The keys to this achievement were the tools that allowed the undeveloped thoughts to emerge—to emerge without fear of criticism or denigration. Metaphorming played a huge role in providing us a mechanism to begin to communicate partially developed ideas. Dialog provided a style of communication that promoted a healthy interaction between team members.

DISCOVERING A CREATIVE WELLSPRING OF IDEAS

It was startling to observe the flow of ideas, proposals, schemes, and opinions that began to flow from the group. We began to focus on new and exciting initiatives, programs, and projects that we elected to undertake in addition to our normal work duties—and we loved it; accomplishment seemed to be the fuel that powered us and set us in motion.

We wanted to tap into the creative power of the subconscious mind. As an experiment, we changed the format of our corporate strategic plan. We believed that rather than spelling out what to do and how to do it in words and text, we would plant strategic thoughts, communicated via pictures and images, throughout the organizations—visual seeds, if you will.

We selected a nautical theme as the metaphor for our strategic plan. We liked this approach because of the similarities between planning and sailing, such as selecting a destination, setting a course, making course adjustments, and winning the race (e.g. the America's cup yacht race). Sailing provided such beautiful images and icons to feed our creative side such as tropical settings, the wind at your face, and gorgeous sunsets.

Our final product was a stunning animated video filled with images, music, and narration. This video set the direction for the organization in a very clear and unforgettable way. The imagery of the America's cup race clearly set a tone of excitement, competition, and urgency. At this point, it was so simple to use the icons of sailboat racing, sleek yachts, the rudder to set the course, the sail to catch the market winds, the anchor to ground us in our values and principles, to invoke the strategies and directions of the plan and establish a call to action.

RESTORING THE VITALITY OF THE GROUP

It was also astounding to watch the vitality of the group and the individual increase. It was as if they had all been given a shot of adrenalin; we were having fun and it was contagious. We wanted to discover how this energy could be bottled and preserved, unleashed when most needed. This book is a result of our desire to impart our experience and share the secrets that we uncovered.

It was now so clear to us the value of maintaining our individual health and wellness. When we felt good, we performed well. We had set in motion core principles that led to tremendous mental well-being. We knew that physical health, personal financial fitness, and harmony in our relationships all contributed to our performance and our personal satisfaction with our work. We came to know that there really is no separation between personal and professional life; there is just life and it is detrimental to try to enforce an artificial separation.

TAKING OWNERSHIP FOR THE WELL-BEING OF THE ORGANIZATION

It is important for team members in *The Quantum Organization* to take full ownership—ownership for their work, their mistakes, their successes, and the well-being of the team and the company. Quma Learning, specifically Steve Chandler, has a saying that we took on as a team, "no one is coming." *No one is coming* to make you happy, *no one is coming* to do your work or fix your problems, and *no one is coming* to make the sale or close the deal for you. You own the problem, you are the problem, and therefore you are the solution.

The key to taking personal ownership is in the language we use and promote. We did not allow *victims* within our midst. As a team, we did not abide excuses for non-performance, such as "Joe did not give me the information in time," "Sally was late," or "Bill was supposed to do it." This is the language of victims not owners. Owners say: "If Joe did not give me the information in time and since this is my problem, what am I going to do to solve it?"

We started to see personal ownership in *The Quantum Organization*, ownership for the health and success of the corporation. One of the personalities that emerged in the group was one of nurturing, a nurturing of the well-being of the company. We took increased ownership of the issues of the corporation. We expanded the scope of our projects, we took a more holistic corporate perspective in all the work that we did. We increased our communication with other groups and teams as we shared our discoveries, thoughts, and ideas.

CHANGING PERSONAL OWNERSHIP

There is a requirement and attending power of personal ownership in delivering a new leadership paradigm. Our team attended a course from Quma Learning entitled the Ownership Spirit. The materials in this course revealed the power in language—the power in positive thinking. Quma taught us about ownership through words that lead to success (owner) instead of words that lead to failure (victim). Examine each of the words or phrases in the table below and think about your state of mind after each. Do you feel a call to action or do you feel hopelessness—a lack of energy?[2]

Table 4.1 Quma Learning's Ownership/Victim Words

Owner	Victim
I want to	I am swamped
Count on me	I should
Count me in	I ought to
What can we do	There is no solution
What else can I do	They're making me do it
When do we start	No one has ever done that
Buy-in	That's not how we do it
Possibility	Restriction
I'll make time	I'm preoccupied
We can make it work	That'll never work

Can you sense the absolute power of taking personal ownership? Do you see the difference ownership language makes in empowering you?

---

2. Quma Learning (1996) *Ownership Spirit.*

Consider the following statements:

1. How in the world will I ever get this project in on time? Jane did not deliver the supply chain process. What is wrong with her? Doesn't she realize how important this is? I don't have the time to do this for her. It will be her fault if this project is incomplete. She has really put me in a bind. There is nothing I can do.
2. This project is due at the end of next week and I have a problem. I need a supply chain process up and running by Wednesday. It does not look like I can count on Jane. What am I going to do about it?

Do you see that statement 2 empowers you to take positive action—to uncover solutions? Statement 1 causes you to think not about solutions but about how you have been victimized by Jane. Words can shape our thoughts; they are a call to action; they are the key to our taking ownership of our work, our relationships, and even our very lives. When you take ownership of problems you empower yourself to find solutions.

THE STRENGTH IN BELIEVING IN EACH OTHER

The real muscle of the group became evident when we were able to trust in the skill and ability of each member of the team. It was this ability to depend on each other that really fueled our independence. As we were able to rely on the other members of the team to do their part and to do it well, we no longer had to waste time and resources in redundant effort. We had an increased expansion of our own ability to get work done, as we were able to trust in others—to economize our knowledge. This trust is a cycle that feeds upon itself, that grows in strength as each team member's skills, self-confidence, and self-image improves.

Chapter 5

A Turning Point:
We Must Invest in People

*THE universe, then, is a unified whole that can to some extent be divided
into separate parts, into objects made of molecules and atoms, themselves
made of particles. But here, at the level of particles, the notion of separate
parts breaks down, the subatomic particles—and therefore, ultimately, all
parts of the universe—cannot be understood as isolated entities but must be
defined through their interrelations.*[1]

INTRODUCTION

In-vest-ment (*in vest' ment*) n. 1. The investment of money or capital in order to gain profitable returns, as interest, income, or appreciation in value. 2. A devoting, using, or giving of time, talent, or
emotional energy, etc., as for a purpose or to achieve something. 3. The
act of investing with quality, etc.[2]

Risk (*risk*), n. 1. Exposure to the chance of injury or loss. 2. The
degree of probability of such loss. 3. To venture upon; to take or run
the chance of.[3]

So what do we risk to venture upon – to take or run the chance of
what? Webster does not give the answer. But let me suggest this conclusion for Webster: to venture upon, to take or run the chance of
greatness, importance, of value. We all have the opportunity to achieve
greatness even if it is only in the eyes of a few, even if we only change
the life of one.

In the course of studying the sciences of the quantum, chaos, and
complexity, we inevitably come across the wonderful quandary of the

1. Fritjof Capra (1988) The Turning Point, Bantam Books, p. 81.
2. Random House Webster's Unabridged Dictionary, 2nd edition, 1999.
3. Ibid.

Butterfly Effect: *Does the flap of a butterfly's wings in Brazil set off a tornado in Texas?*[4] This phenomenon is a study in nonlinear equations. Nonlinear systems are foundational to chaos theory and often show signs of exceptionally unique and complex characteristics each time they are solved. As with the butterfly, can we really determine what is the long-term impact of the changes we make in our small corner of the world—of our implementation as *The Quantum Organization*?

And in the same spirit as the Butterfly Effect, you will probably recall the famous compound interest story about the Emperor of China who offered the inventor of the game of chess one wish. The inventor replied that he wanted one grain of rice on square one of the chess-board, two grains on the second square, four on the third and so on through square sixty-four. The unsuspecting emperor agreed to the seemingly humble request. But two raised to the sixty-fourth power is eighteen million trillion grains of rice—more than all the rice in China. The skillful inventor did not obtain all the rice in China; he did how-ever loose his head.

Ralph Waldo Emerson helps us understand the tremendous poten-tial in all of us:

The creation of a thousand forests is in one acorn.[5]

Let me introduce you to one such acorn, Ken McCumber. I have known Ken for many years and consider him one of my closest friends. I have had many occasions to observe him both in professional and social settings. When we first met my assessment of Ken was that he was obviously bright, but he was an underachiever—an underachiever in the sense that he routinely placed artificial barriers to his progression in his way. In retrospect, I believe Ken was, like so many of us, a prod-uct of a professional way of life that relegated him to a specific loca-tion in the corporate food chain. Along with that spot in the food chain came a very restricted set of expectations and perhaps most damaging of all was a collection of limitations—limitations in the sense of the quality of his ideas, the value of his work, and even the level of his intelligence. It seemed that where we worked (perhaps your workplace is different), one's level in the organization was the real measure of value and contribution instead of what you really knew or even what you did.

Professionally, I observed Ken from a distance for the first five years of our association, until in 1999 I had the opportunity to bring

4. The Butterfly Effect is attributed to Edward Lorenz, a mathematician at the Massachusetts Institute of Technology.
5. Emerson, http://www.gocreate.com/QuotAmaze

him into our workgroup. Ken brought with him a powerful resentment of the corporation's failure to act, to act upon his ideas, and to afford him the respect he felt he was due as an individual contributor in the company. In a word, Ken was a victim—a victim of his own failure to rise above the corporate culture and take responsibility for his own success.

To his credit, Ken took to our new culture as the proverbial duck takes to water. Ken played a huge role in the development and implementation of our quantum ideas. What was the most startling, however, was his personal transformation from a victim of the oppressive corporate apparatus to the owner of his success. I might even say that Ken's makeover may have been the greatest single accomplishment of all our efforts. Ken went on to become a key officer in a competitive telecommunications start-up company. To this day, he is a committed advocate of creativity, dialog, and learning in the workplace—and in all aspects of life. Ken is a teacher at heart—he has taught many the power and worth of quantum concepts. He has touched the lives of hundreds of people for the better—he has made an investment in people.

Do we really have any idea of the long-term and far-reaching impacts of our work—of the seeds we sow? As with the Butterfly Effect or the compound interest story, we may be responsible for spectacular global changes through the small things we do, by investing in the individual—by valuing people. In chapters 1 and 3 we were introduced to the concept of strange attractors. Strange attractor is the name scientists have affixed to those few fundamental principles that drive complex systems. Do you remember our tree metaphor in chapter 3? We discussed that attempting to manage the health and well-being of every leaf and branch individually would be a hopeless exercise in ineffectiveness. However, if we attend to the roots of the tree, the leaves and branches will emerge with form and beauty. So how do we apply this principle of strange attractor in the workplace—with people? Let me suggest this by way of example: instead of managing the project we attend to the needs of the people—instead of supervising we lead; rather than coaching we participate together—we learn from each other; in place of empowering we share power—rather than talking we listen; as an alternative to being served we serve others.

VALUE INVESTING

Value investing is the name for the technique of choosing investments on the basis of their essential value—finding the golden nuggets that are otherwise hidden from view. So it is with people. As leaders we must know the people we work with. We must become familiar with their diverse talents—their uniqueness.

There is power in diversity, as I discovered several years ago. In 1983 I found myself working in Albuquerque, New Mexico, in the information systems (IS) business. We were building and staffing a new $100,000,000 data center. The job pool of computer workers and programmers in Albuquerque was pretty much exhausted at that time. In order to meet our burgeoning need for top IS professionals we had to carry out a nationwide search. We brought in top talent from all parts of the country. We ended up with teams of experts with a marvelous blend of experiential, cultural, and ethnic backgrounds—we had a truly diverse lineup.

We established learning teams to collect and glean as much of the knowledge and experience as possible from our new squad. One of the valuable outcomes from our learning teams was revealed when we conducted a re-examination of our processes. We combed through our procedures and methods with relentless zeal uncovering opportunities for improvement almost at every turn. These opportunities took the form of eliminating rework (quality improvement), eliminating work that was no longer of value, uncovering skills deficiencies, and implementing training programs to bring our staff up to speed, establishing repeatable processes (software development, scheduling, program and project management) that eliminated waste, and more. We were able to save money by stabilizing our workforce; we were able to get more work done with the same number of people. We were able to increase our management span of control by making our process more error free and more effective.

It was such a testimony of the value and might of a diverse work team—diverse in experience, knowledge, and perspective. It was also a very unassailable revelation in terms of the harm caused by a homogeneous and somewhat uniform workgroup. Without the assorted points of view our new team had just acquired we were blind to the possibilities. This experience alone moved us to insure that each of our workgroup's make-up was loaded with an assortment of people, skills, and experience.

It was also obvious that in order to take full advantage of these new teams, we had to spend time together in dialog. We took every opportunity to bring the team(s) together in dialog—formal and informal. These dialog sessions were fertile ground for pop-up leadership opportunities. When someone had an observable affinity for an issue or project they emerged to lead the team. In the fifteen years that I had spent in the industry I had never been a part of a more creative, energetic, motivated, and truly happy workgroup. Our productivity soared—the new creative ideas flowed like water—we all loved our work and it showed. We had experienced the thrill of true diversity—not some farce of a governmental program lacking in spirit and character—focusing on the superficial.

In the latter years of the 20th century, society, in my opinion, incorrectly labeled programs like Affirmative Action as diversity programs. While these programs were important in raising our awareness and setting the stage for true diversity in the workplace, they are not in and of themselves the end point. There is amazing power and importance in bringing diverse experiences, viewpoints, skills, talents, and abilities to the corporate table. It is time for us to move on—to move past these outdated administrative programs, and to experience the value of true diversity.

So how do we start? One way is to take personal responsibility to convey what value we individually bring to the table. Simply put, why should a place be saved for us at the table at all? Surely not because of the color of our skin, but because of the rich experiences that are our heritage—that make us unique, that make us who we are; because of our talents, our training, our skills, our education—all born out of hard work and effort.

So what really is our investment? It is money, materials, and our time; we invest in training the correct principles and doing it with quality. We make investments in ourselves as we change our own personal paradigms—as we walk our talk. We take risks and we protect others as they work at changing the heart and mind of the organization. In other words, we invest in people—we invest in change.

CHANGING THE CULTURE

The challenges of taking on the "corporate culture" are not insignificant. Many a good person has gone down with his ship trying to sail over that corporate reef. Simply put, there are roadblocks (and solutions) ahead for the managers that want to change the outdated paradigms of corporate America. The most difficult of challenges is that of overcoming the conventional management wisdom. The further up the management chain you go the more entrenched the conventional management paradigm. After all, these corporate giants rose to the top of the greatest companies in America on the back of Newtonian mechanistic thinking. But like any pyramidal system, current hierarchical styles tend to benefit those at the top much more than those of us at the bottom.

We knew that the old traditions must change so we made a short list of some of the key characteristics of our new culture:

- We must nurture a culture of risk takers—people who understand and believe in the usefulness of failure and of learning from all our experiences.
- Our new order ought to reward risk-takers and learners instead of punishing those who make justifiable mistakes.
- We should encourage participation by all—at every level (I hate that word) of the organization.
- Anyone in the organization, regardless of their role, should be allowed to "stop the train" when necessary; each person has a responsibility to hold up production when they see a problem or an opportunity.
- We must look for occasions to use creative techniques and tools in everything we do, including meetings, presentations, brainstorming, proposals, advertising and marketing, manufacturing and production, reading, writing, and learning.
- It is critical that we develop and foster an atmosphere of dialog— we must spend more time than ever before in conversation with people.
- Finally and perhaps most importantly, each of us must demand true diversity in the workplace; it is the right thing to do for the business and it is the right thing to do for the people.

So how did we overcome the existing culture, contain the inertia, and build a new standard to work and live by?

1. To start we recruited an executive sponsor—we used him to help define and promote *The Quantum Organization.*
2. We selected one that was forward thinking and demonstrated some entrepreneurial spirit.
3. We put together a sales plan as we would with any customer or account.
   a. Prepared a presentation with a benefit statement.
   b. Developed a timeline with milestones and resources required.
   c. Identified who might be the stakeholders.
   d. Defined the role we wanted the sponsor to play.
   e. Acknowledged the risks—to the company and to the sponsor.
   f. Quantified outcomes and the return on investment.

Our sponsor was good and quite helpful, but there was still a significant amount of work to do for the rest of us. Within the scope of our management assignments we worked laterally within the organization. We dusted off our executive sales presentation and worked it with peers; we worked at plus or minus one level within the organization. We worked with suppliers and vendors and required them to use *Quantum Organizational* techniques in order to work with us.

We had five objectives and tactics we used when working with peer groups.

1. It was our objective to educate and inform first, last, and always. Many on our team dedicated a significant amount of time giving presentations, responding to questions, and attending staff meetings.
2. We knew that if we could get individuals and teams to participate— to give our concepts a try—we could win them over. We conducted workshops and role-playing sessions with several peer groups. In every case and almost to the last person these were successful in demonstrating the usefulness of quantum concepts.
3. Our third objective was to convert people to our view of leadership. We believed that if our work was true, and if it was going to spread, it needed a base of faithful converts. This was a sales process just like any other. We worked to close every deal; and no deal was complete until we had convinced our peer(s) of the worth of quantum concepts.
4. We also believed that just like any new doctrine, new converts were going to require ongoing support—support in the sense of retraining, dialog sessions, and political backing. We established a network of supporters, we defended one another's agendas, we attended each other's meetings, we invited new converts to be stakeholders and subject matter experts for new leadership curricula, and we were good listeners.
5. Finally, we knew that we had only scratched the surface in our learning. We wanted to continue to grow intellectually—we wanted to insure that we had a forum for continued exploration of new ideas and the building of a knowledge base that would allow us to challenge the prevailing thinking. So we created learning teams and we invited the best and brightest we could find—we explored, we challenged, and we experimented.

We surrounded ourselves with positive affirmations. We changed our websites, business cards, letterhead, plaques, brochures, and e-mail to include encouraging phrases and pictures that helped us keep our message and our goals at the forefront of our minds. These phrases and declarations delivered positive returns in the following ways:

- They helped us to keep a focus on the changes that we needed to make in our organization. Keeping the terms, language, and phrases of *The Quantum Organization* always in front of us resulted in a rapid adoption of the strategies and system of beliefs that we knew were important to our success and well-being.
- Keeping the tenets of the strategy in front of us caused us to continue to ponder and question the validity of our approach. Since just about every document or online visual representation or text included a pronouncement of our new beliefs, we were constantly challenging ourselves regarding our definitions, our values, and our true commitment to this new way of thinking. This resulted in a refinement of our beliefs and a deeper devotion to them.
- Our communications outside our team (i.e. customers, colleagues, vendors) caused quite a stir of interest. We answered many questions regarding what changes we were implementing. This not only helped us clarify our own thinking, but we gained many disciples as well.

We put together a team project to write an ebook on the new management process. It is a proven and well-known fact that writing and teaching new principles are the best tools available to reinforce learning; writing about a topic is the most powerful means we have to help define and clarify our thinking. The better informed, prepared, and indoctrinated we were the better we were at communicating our message. This led to increased credibility and our credibility was key to our ongoing success.

The ebook project was one of the most profound learning experiences of all on the topic of the new leadership. We felt that a handbook of instructions or an inspirational guide to the concepts of the creative and the quantum would be a wonderful tool to shore up our message. What it became was a powerful forum for dialog on the nuances and details of our thinking—of our concepts and principles. The exercise of writing the ebook ignited our creative fires; it caused us to focus our thinking and give the clarity of thought required to be able to educate others and guide them to our way of thinking. We engaged in many dialog sessions, we conducted research, and we experimented with the concepts. While we were unable to complete the ebook for various and sundry reasons, this book, *The Quantum Advantage,* is a more comprehensive outgrowth of that project.

Finally, nothing is a more powerful reason for change than good performance and we know that imitation is the highest form of flattery. Our message to our peers was: implement *The Quantum Organization* at whatever level that you can and start to enjoy the increased benefits as quickly as possible. We told them not to let a minute go by when they were not communicating the value and benefits that they were seeing. However, we found that the best advertisement was the people on the team—these were the best evangelists.

We had a very enlightening experience while presenting a business strategy plan to our executive leadership team. Several of our team had a part in the presentation. The enthusiasm and passion was so obvious that members of the leadership team noticed and commented on it. Almost in unison the group began to extol their love for their work, their eagerness to begin each day, and the bonds that were created between one another. The looks on the faces of the executives were priceless—they wanted to know more—they wanted to know how we did it.

Once we truly understand and experience the power of *The Quantum Organization* we can never really go back to the previous style. There will be a lot of resistance. In the wee hours of the night we may begin to question whether it is possible to make real change—even whether it is worth it. But like any revolution, it is given life by way of a thought or an idea in the hearts of passionate people who want to make a difference. William Jennings Bryan put it this way:

> Destiny is no matter of chance. It is a matter of choice: It is not a thing to be waited for; it is a thing to be achieved.[6]

CHANGING OUR NOTION OF RISK

It is critical that a manager surround himself or herself with good people, bright, intelligent people that have a good self-image and are willing to take on and slay the corporate goliaths. The risks of taking on the corporate "wisdom" can be significant. We risk reputations, careers, compensation, our very jobs, self-respect, and self-esteem. What we found is that the fear of risk fades. We discovered that the risk of doing nothing is greater than the risk of action—the risk of not being true to one's nature.

Maslow helps us to understand our need for self-actualization and personal fulfillment in his famous hierarchy of needs. Dr. Abraham Maslow developed a theory of motivation describing the process by which an individual progresses from basic needs to the highest needs of what he called self-actualization—the fulfillment of one's greatest human potential.

The message in this pyramid is that once we have satisfied our need

6. William Jennings Bryan, http://quotationpage.com/quotes/William_Jennings_Bryan

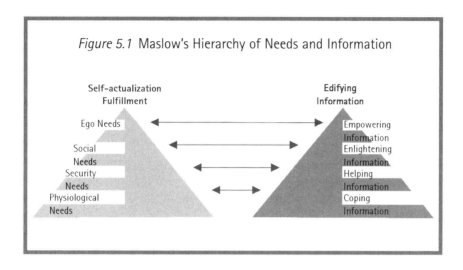

Figure 5.1 Maslow's Hierarchy of Needs and Information

for security, or, in other words, once we are secure in our employment and secure in who we are, we begin to satisfy our more social needs— our need for enlightenment. It is at this point that a team is primed and ready to take on the corporate culture—to slay the corporate goliaths— to take the risks. Maslow tells us that this is when the search for enlightenment becomes a need and not some ethereal vision to be hoped for but not achieved. This is when the principles of *The Quantum Organization* are so compelling that risks to career and professional reputation seem trivial compared to the risk of not being true to oneself.

You remember Ken, our acorn from earlier in the chapter. He is an example of moving oneself towards enlightenment. Ken no longer views the quantum concepts as wants—to him they are needs. He looks for opportunities to incorporate these precepts everywhere he goes and with everyone he meets. He refuses to follow willingly anyone who is still operating under the outdated mechanistic paradigms. Ken loves these concepts and he gains energy from them. He has felt the regenerative powers of the quantum and views them as vital to his physical and mental well-being.

FOCUSING ON RELATIONSHIPS

Quantum science tells us that the most important things in nature, therefore the most important things in our nature, are relationships. Experiments were conducted to determine if paired electrons would exhibit, at a distance, the same characteristics they display when side by side. Simply put, these experiments would prove if relationships exist between elementary particles in nature.

Frenchman Alaine Aspect conducted experiments with paired electrons. The twin electron, confirming quantum theory expectations and demonstrating that there are relationships that endure over distance, reflected whatever you did to the first electron. This work proved that paired electrons remained in a relationship and reacted to one another even though separated by distance; it proved that the foundational elements of the universe form and are in relationships one with another.

Relationships between people are born and nurtured out of dialog—out of quality interactions one with another. Dialog is key to building and maintaining relationships—dialog is impossible without relationships. So what is dialog? The great physicist David Bohm gives us his definition:

> We need to be able to communicate freely in a creative movement in which no one permanently holds to or otherwise defends his (or her) own ideas...Discussion is almost like a ping-pong game, where people are batting the ideas back and forth and the object of the game is to win or to get points for yourself...In dialog, however, nobody is trying to win. Everybody wins if anybody wins.[7]

"Everybody wins if anybody wins." What a powerful and liberating statement. This is the only foundation possible for building relationships in *The Quantum Organization.*

What you will uncover as you begin your search for *The Quantum Organization* is that the most valued treasures in all of life are relationships; so it stands to reason that you must put your maximum effort into building them. Relationships are the source of intellectual growth and stimulation. The source of joy and happiness is sharing with and serving others. This includes not only your peers and associates in the organizations, but your leaders as well. Robert K. Greenleaf, noted author and lecturer, spent much of his life studying management, organizations, and leadership. He is the developer of the theory of Servant Leadership. This theory has a focus of service to others, sharing power (participative management), and building a sense of community in the workplace. Greenleaf states that:

> A new moral principle is emerging which holds that the only authority deserving one's allegiance is that which is free and knowingly granted by the led to the leader in response to, and in proportion to, the clearly evident servant stature of the leader...Those who choose to follow this principle will not casually accept the authority of existing

7. David Bohm (1996) *On Dialogue,* Routledge, p. 4.

institutions. Rather, they will freely respond only to individuals who are chosen as leaders because they are proven and trusted servants.[8]

Greenleaf says that we can, and I think have a moral obligation to, freely follow only servant leaders.

As we build respectful relationships amongst our peers and associates, we must also demand the same from our leadership. *The Quantum Organization*'s cornerstone principle is relationships; that is, quality relationships built upon a foundation of trust, dialog, respect, sharing, service, equality, ownership, and thoughtfulness.

TRAINING AND LEARNING ORGANIZATIONS

John Stuart Mill was born 20 May 1806 the eldest son of James Mill. Many regard Mill as one of the great thinkers in history. Quite an honor given that almost exclusively his father, James Mill, educated him. James Mill's objective was to make his son's mind an unparalleled engine of thought. It seems that he succeeded. John Stuart Mill's work included treatises on a variety of subjects including economics and philosophy. Many of his essays on religion, economics, politics, and logic have become landmark works that have stood the test of time. Mill was a genius with depth and breadth of wisdom and experience. He gives us some insight to learning—to knowing—in the following quote:

> The only way in which a human being can make some approach to knowing the whole of a subject is by hearing what can be said about it by persons of every variety of opinion and studying all modes in which it can be looked at by every character of mind. No wise man ever acquired his wisdom in any mode but this.[9]

John Stuart Mill gives us great evidence that dialog is critical, perhaps foundational, to real learning, to real wisdom. We are referring to content rich dialog, laden with opinion by "every character of mind."

In the end the key to benefits of *The Quantum Organization* is people—finding ways of tapping into the vast capabilities within us all. Our management practices have truly quelled the means to our true nature; blocking us from seeing our path to a greatness that, viewed through the mechanistic lenses of our time, is blurred and nondescript.

8. Robert K. Greenleaf (1977) *Servant Leadership*, Paulist Press, p. 10.
9. John Stuart Mill, in Robert L. Heilbroner (1992) *The Worldly Philosophers*, Blackstone Audio Books.

But there is no doubt about it—the key to this untouched potential is people. There is no new fad management technique that will give managers access to this potential. We must unleash the natural power and capabilities that are trapped within people—in short management must get out of the way of staff. Management's new job is to remove the organizational pebbles from the path of our teams.

Chapter 6

A Transformation:
Delivering a Return on Investment

WHEN I heard the learned astronomer; when the proofs, the figures, were ranged in columns before me; when I was shown the charts and diagrams, to add, divide, and measure them; when I, sitting, heard the astronomer, when he lectured with much applause in the lecture room, how soon, unaccountable, I became tired and sick; 'till rising and gliding out, I wander'd off by myself, in the mystical moist night-air, and from time to time, looked up in perfect silence at the stars.[1]

INTRODUCTION

In today's economic state of affairs companies are pinching pennies harder then ever. To get budget money for restructuring, reengineering, training, or even value creation is like pulling teeth. Not only that, if you are spending any significant time on projects falling outside of the core business you are more than likely going to find yourself looking for a job.

The irony in all of this is that many of the items just identified (value creation, training, restructuring) are the key to productivity and growth. Tying the value of *The Quantum Organization* to the corporate bottom line is essential to upper management support and to the assignment of budget dollars. Defining a very specific return on investment (ROI) from *The Quantum Organization* is sometimes difficult to quantify in traditional terms, nevertheless you will find most upper management teams require it.

Many *Quantum Organization* purists resist putting what they consider to be the customary restraints and blinders of metrics and measurements upon this new leadership style. Metrics tend to stifle

1. Walt Whitman, www.bartleby.com

spontaneity and creativity. In the quantum world matter can exist as either a particle or a wave. When you measure for the particle you miss the wave—when you measure for the wave you miss the particle. This line of thinking is easy to defend and a multitude of examples can be given that demonstrate the creative blackout that occurs when we create hard boundaries in our thinking by dictating process and measuring for a specific output.

If you remember our dialog vs debate discussion in chapter 3, we said that debate kills creativity because it makes no allowance for an alternative or better solution. In the process of debate you must have a winner and loser. In *The Quantum Organization* measurements and metrics take on many of the same characteristics as debate. Strict measurements cause one to seek the ideal process, ideal in the sense that the measurements come out the best—there must be a winner and loser. Essentially measuring makes no real allowance for radical deviation from that process—no substantial creative innovation.

Some might argue that process improvement engineers dedicate their very existence to tweaking the practice at every junction and joint—continuing to rummage around for that elusive morsel of incremental efficiency—Kaizen. Kaizen is a word the Japanese use that describes a gradual and ordered continuous improvement process. This concept embodies the notion of small steps—it assumes the foundation upon which the process is built is sound and merely needs to be squeezed and pinched on a continuous basis to reap great rewards—some certain improvements maybe; great rewards never. A real-life example of Kaizen in action might help us visualize how this concept might work in our world.

As part of the Bell System I had much experience with a concept called the Bell System Practice. This was an enormous set of office procedures (OP) designed by efficiency experts after years of experience with continual improvement. Of course the focus was to create efficient workers and not necessarily to foster independence, creativity, innovation, or breakthrough thinking. One such OP described how to arrange a worker's desk for maximum efficiency in stapling papers and delivering them to the outbox for release to the next phase of the process. Detailed in this guide were recommended locations on the desktop for papers, stapler, and outbox. There were layouts for left-handed people and right-handed people. The OP even went into mind-numbing detail on the proper procedure for retrieving the papers from the paper pile, inserting them into the stapler, reminders to keep your fingers out from under the maw of the stapler, and finally steps for placing the stapled forms into the outbox.

Is this story a little outrageous? Maybe, but millions of Bell System employees aren't laughing. Regardless of what you might think of the story it does help to illustrate the creative collapse that occurs when a rigid process is substituted for free agency—when we allow process engineers to do our thinking for us. To be fair to the principles of Kaizen we must disclose that Kaizen does make provisions for some innovation. However, it refers to those activities as initiated by senior management and includes things like buying new machinery, opening new markets, and changing strategies.

So how do we know *The Quantum Organization* is better? How do we satisfy the demand by senior management for a clear set of steps to a satisfactory return on investment?

VALUE INNOVATION

One of the tactics that helped us bring into view an ROI program was "Value Innovation." Value Innovation is a concept based on the notion of rendering the competition irrelevant to your business. In other words, using bursts of creative insight to leapfrog the competition by delivering products and services that are so superior to what exists on the market, you cause the competition to be of no consequence. This process is completely foreign to most process-improvement engineers and traditional competitive analysts.

W. Chan Kim and Renée Mauborgne of MIT developed the concept of Value Innovation. They help us understand the differences between typical competitive strategy and Value Innovation:

> Managers typically assess what competitors do and strive to do it better. Using this approach, companies expend tremendous effort and achieve only incremental improvement—imitation—not innovation. By focusing on the competition, companies tend to be reactive, and their understanding of emerging mass markets and changing customer demands becomes hazy.[2]

This concept also parallels continuous improvement programs. When we only focus on doing what we are doing—doing what we have always done—we will never break out of our box and see the possibilities.

They go on to describe value innovation this way:

> To value innovate, managers must ask two questions: Is the firm offering customers radically superior value? And is the firm's price level

2. W. Chan Kim and Renée Mauborgne (1999) *Strategy, Value Innovation, and the Knowledge Economy*, MIT, p. 3.

accessible to the mass of buyers in the target market? A consequence
of market insight gained from creative strategic thinking, value innovation focuses on redefining problems to shift the performance criteria that matter to customers.[3]

Kim and Mauborgne give a very good example of how Callaway Golf
used value innovation to transform the golf club market:

> Callaway Golf, the US golf club manufacturer, which in 1991 launched
> its "Big Bertha" golf club. The product rapidly rose to dominate the
> market, wresting market share from its rivals and expanding the total
> golf club market. Despite intense competition, Callaway did not focus
> on its competitors. Rival golf clubs looked alike and featured sophisti-
> cated enhancements, a result of attentive benchmarking of the com-
> petitor's products.[4]

Callaway spent time understanding why non-golfers do not play the
game. They found that the thought of hitting a tiny ball with a little
club head was too intimidating for many people. The introduction of
the Big Bertha golf club met a pent-up demand for a product that
would make golf more fun for a large unserved segment of the market. As a result Callaway transformed the marketplace forever and literally rendered their competition irrelevant—at least for a time.

Value Innovation in *The Quantum Organization* delivers a significant return on investment. *The Quantum Organization* delivers many
powerful tools to assist in the creative process as we have discussed.
Value Innovation in *The Quantum Organization* is a combination of
those creative tools and an emphasis on delivering value to the buyer
instead of a myopic focus on outdoing the competition.[5]

THE IMPORTANCE OF JOB SATISFACTION

We have already considered how employee job satisfaction is critical
to business success—through increased self-esteem, self-fulfillment,
and a balanced approach to life. These are all difficult concepts to
build an ROI plan around—or are they?

Most recognized experts in human resource management continue

3. Ibid., p. 7.
4. Ibid., p. 5.
5. Author's note: As part of the creative and innovation process, a business must have
    the necessary skills, abilities, and infrastructure in place to execute on its business
    plan. This includes the core business functions as well as any new projects that may
    come up. The failure to build the supporting capabilities to support the business plan
    is a sure recipe for disappointment.

to advocate the classic management and leadership rhetoric that many of us have heard time immemorial. These include the threadbare concepts of:

1. Coaching.
2. Productive use of strengths.
3. Management by objective.
4. Process improvement.
5. Manage by walking around.
6. Dress for success.
7. Empowerment.
8. Total Quality Management.
9. Kaizen.
10. Measure, analyze, improve, and control.

One way to summarize these and many more of the classic management idiom is *a pigeonhole for everyone and everyone in their pigeonhole.* These concepts are the model of the machine—of a manageable and well-ordered universe where everything is predetermined; predestined to a foreordained outcome.

> My job satisfaction does not stem from tucking me away in some well-ordered corner loaded with inveterate tasks that make productive use of my strengths. How and when do I get to learn something new—how do I test my wings—when do I create? I will not respond to being measured, analyzed, improved, and controlled. I know that my universe is not manageable using Newtonian mechanistic routines. The universe is not a thing to be tamed; it is living organism to be explored, to be appreciated, and to be experienced.

Job satisfaction is directly tied to individual self-image and self-esteem. The renowned expert Dr. Nathaniel Branden tells us this regarding self-esteem and its importance:

> Of all the judgments we pass in life, none is as important as the one we pass on ourselves. Nearly every psychological problem – from anxiety and depression to self-sabotage at work or at school, from fear of intimacy to chronic hostility – is traceable to low self-esteem. In the chaotic and competitive world we face today, both personal happiness and economic survival rest on how well we understand self-esteem and nurture it in ourselves and in others...While poor self-esteem often undercuts the capacity for real accomplishment, even among the most

talented, it does not necessarily do so. What is far more certain is that it undercuts the capacity for satisfaction.[6]

Dr. Branden also tells us that self-esteem is directly tied to accomplishment. He explains that a culture of self-esteem and personal accountability is essential to business success and perhaps even to business survival.

The satisfaction one gets from associations with co-workers and peers, relationships with superiors, having meaningful work, sharing responsibility, personal accountability, and accomplishment leads to increased self-esteem and improved self-image. Self-esteem, or a sense of accomplishment, personal growth, and integrity, is directly related to productivity and the satisfaction one gets from work. An effective ROI plan must include a component of job satisfaction. So how do we determine job satisfaction? Ask the people. Build comprehensive surveys—listen to what the employees are saying—use open-ended questions. Change the surveys and ask them again, and again, and again.

THE REWARDS OF JOB SATISFACTION

The depth and quality of job satisfaction can determine whether an organization will lead its market—will value innovate, or merely trail the competition—continuing that incremental competitive squabble that nearly cost companies like Compaq their very existence.

A recent nationwide job satisfaction study conducted by Bavendam Research indicates that the number one driver for satisfaction in a job is opportunity. In other words, people derive satisfaction from their jobs when they have challenging prospects at work. This includes the possibility for additional responsibility—a sharing of authority and managerial power, participation in new and exciting projects, special assignments, and leadership opportunities.[7]

So if a company takes the time and effort to provide opportunity for employees, what is the return on investment? We can characterize the yield in terms of soft returns, things like loyalty, creativity, harmony in the workplace, service, sharing, etc. The hard returns are improved customer service ratings, sales and profits, reduced absenteeism, reduced complaints and grievances, headcount reductions, etc.

WHAT ARE THE SOFT RETURNS?

The soft returns are the most difficult to quantify and generally are not

6. Nathaniel Branden (1994) *Six Pillars of Self-Esteem*, Bantam, p. 40.
7. Bavendam Research Incorporated (2000) *Managing Job Satisfaction*.

enough to elicit budget dollars even from the most generous of keepers of the corporate purse. But anyone who has ever led a group of people knows how valuable and how tangible they are. Sometimes called soft skills or even people skills, affixing a value to these talents has eluded traditional organizations since that apple was eaten in a certain garden.

Let me by way of example show soft returns in an actual *Quantum Organization*—our Wholesale Strategy team. We have discussed this merry band before in chapter 3—the group of twenty or so marketing, training, financial, and forecasting professionals.

I will begin with a small account of how this team was formed—how we came together in the first place. First let me say that the terms "strategy" and "wholesale operations" were never mentioned in the same sentence before our team was created. This was a very traditional and core operation in the telecommunications industry; made up of some very traditional thinkers. However, we were fortunate to have a few more open-minded sages sprinkled throughout the leadership team and within the ranks as well.

The strategy team coalesced as a product of splintered organizations, early retirements, and some reengineering within the wholesale operation. Simply put, we were a group of nomads and itinerant castoffs that was supposed to come together and drive the strategic vision of a $3 billion business unit. I don't want to give the impression that the individuals were not intelligent and promising souls with potential—they were some of the best and brightest people I have ever worked with.

What made this group such a wonderful collection was its rich diversity of background, culture, style, and education. As I contemplated the paradox of how this group came together—some of the best and brightest viewed as hand-me-downs—given up to this new ethereal strategy organization without so much as a whimper of protest, it became clear to me that the larger organization suffered from a very myopic and filtered bias with regard to people. What made this moment all the more ironic is that the telecommunications industry was probably unparalleled in its support of governmental affirmative action programs.

The soft returns from *The Quantum Organization* were real, they energized our team, and they provided a spark that ignited a burst of curiosity and creativity throughout the entire organization. These returns came in the form of:

- *Better Teamwork*: my observations of a two-year period clearly indicated that our team worked better together than before we implemented the doctrine of *The Quantum Organization.* Our meetings were more energetic, there was more help and support for teammates, and meetings were more productive and efficient.

- *Improved Ideas:* using the new tools from our toolbox we generated materially more and better ideas and solutions to problems, product development, market management, and strategic plan development.
- *Improved Individual Self-esteem:* as I observed each of the team members individually it was crystal clear that after introducing the principles of *The Quantum Organization* the employees were happier, more confident, enjoyed learning much more, were more respectful of others, and their individual performance ratings improved across the board.
- *Better Customer Relationships:* improved relationships with teammates translated directly to the interactions the team had with customers, both internal and external. Customer feedback improved and while we had several initiatives in place to improve customer satisfaction, we felt strongly that our outlook and attitudes contributed to the success with our customers.

Though in the end new products, new revenues, and greater profits are the ultimate deliverable back to the company, we know that in order to achieve these hard returns people must be part of a respectful and nurturing environment—just like any living creature we are at our best when we are cared for and appreciated.

Building Loyalty

One of the principal drags on productivity is employee turnover—the constant expense and overhead of finding and training good people. While in *The Quantum Organization* a little planned chaos keeps us on our toes, the hemorrhaging of the best and brightest of our people is devastating. And as any manager knows, it is never the more readily replaceable of the team that leaves—it is only the ones that can leave—the ones that other organizations and companies want—the ones you cannot afford to loose.

Now let me make myself perfectly clear on the subject of people and their various talents. In *The Quantum Organization* everyone plays an important role in weaving our diverse human tapestry so fundamental to true diversity. We have all been endowed with a unique variety of talents and gifts—each an important contribution to the greater good. Yet, some of these gifts are found in greater abundance in the world than others. Some talents are more difficult to cultivate and therefore are more rare and certainly harder to recruit and keep.

In our *Quantum Organization* not only did we never loose a single person to outside recruiting (internal or external to the company), we had an enormous number of requests to join our team—when people truly understood what we were about they were clamoring to be a part of our team. This was not a loyalty to a dynamic leader but an allegiance to a belief—to a cause—to principles that rang true to the very souls of our humanity. What people were experiencing was just right and good; and the loyalty we experienced was a loyalty to ourselves—to our very nature.

Building Commitment

There is nothing more frustrating and less rewarding than working with uncommitted people. They do a great job of disguising themselves but you know of whom I speak—the ones that never volunteer for the tough assignment, rarely have a new and exciting idea, and are never around when the time-critical assignment comes in at 4.30pm.

Not so within *The Quantum Organization*. Our group assumed responsibility for the success of the company. Now some might say that in order to make any real difference on a company-wide scale significant authority and scope of responsibility is required. Perhaps there is some truth to that belief if taking a very narrow and mechanistic viewpoint. What we experienced was individuals taking a very holistic perspective regarding their jobs, their accountability, and the scope of their influence—we were casting a pretty wide net with regard to what we were committed to do to contribute to the success of the company—if we could help we got involved. As a group we were an exciting and unpredictable bunch to be around. Many, many new ideas would spring forth every time two or more of us gathered together.

Giving Service

One of the marvelous benefits—a blessing really—was the commitment to serve one another. It was a commitment to the welfare and benefit of each individual on the team. We were really able to glory in the successes of others and share the sorrow in their losses. Gone was the petty competitiveness that often invades more conventional organizations.

It was a moving sight to see the participation we all shared in each other's personal as well as professional lives (or again is it just life?). We helped on projects at work, we helped people move their homes, and we even stood by one of our own through a painful divorce. The thought of undermining a teammate in order to feather our own nest was offensive to us all. We shared our work as well as our rewards— we truly were a family.

Sharing with the Team

When I think of sharing my mind goes to a certain corporate executive strategist the company hired about the time our wholesale strategy team came into being. As a team, we watched this guy function with total awe and disbelief. What we were watching was the worst example of sharing and teamwork possible within the bounds of the law. The pattern was clear; this chap started out building plans and strategies while locked within the walls of his office on the 52nd floor. You could almost measure the brainwaves as they emanated from his better-than-average intellect. You could see it on his face every time he emerged from his office—he had all the answers—he knew what needed to be done.

As time went by (we will call our chief strategist Rick), Rick entered into phase two of the standard Chief Strategy Officer progression (perhaps deterioration is a better word)—he started to produce thick white binders full of all of his good ideas. He had graphs and charts, quotes, and references; he had primary research and secondary data; it was time to share all of his good thoughts with us and change our world for the better.

The hell of it all for this guy was none of us were interested—60,000 employees and no one cared what he had in the binders. Of course no one was asked for any input into his work either—perhaps there is a correlation lurking here?

Well, on the road he went. He hopped from city to city, from corporate headquarters, to regional centers, to branch offices. He had a good story, his presentation skills were matchless—no one was listening. After a disappointing six weeks of road shows we find our hero back in his corner office, shades drawn, brain output a shadow of its former volume. It was beginning to dawn on him that he was in trouble. He was being paid a high salary and correspondingly the company's expectations were high—what was he to do?

This is phase three, affectionately known as the hoarding phase. Rick began to fear for his job. It was a good job and he did not want to lose it. He reasoned that there was power in the information and wisdom in his thick three-ring binders. He came to the conclusion that he would hoard the data and only share it in meetings with the boss and other movers and shakers of the company. Surely they would see how valuable he was—how wise and knowledgeable he was—how they could not do without him. Four weeks later Rick was looking for work.

The moral of this sad but all too true story is that the power of knowledge/information/data is in the sharing. Data are like rabbits—you start with a little and eventually you get a lot. Rick's story is not an isolated or uncommon story. In fact in our case, Rick was the third such strategic savior the company had hired in as many years. Rick's problems did not start in phase three (the hoarding phase); they started at the beginning when Rick failed to share the potential rewards and recognition for the development of a corporate strategic plan, when he chose not to include the stakeholders from across the company, when he made the mistake of thinking that his intellect was greater than the group's.

Our thanks go to Rick for helping us clarify our vision of sharing power, sharing data, and sharing rewards and recognition. Our own experience with dialog, goal setting, and metaphorming—giving service, being loyal and committed to the common good cemented in our minds the power of sharing—the power of inclusion—the power of teams.

Engaging People in Meaningful Work

An important focus of *The Quantum Organization* is the assurance that everyone is engaged in meaningful work—work that contributes towards the shared goals of the team—labor that is challenging and vital. Also, these are endeavors that ultimately help to make the world a better place. This is the building of products and services that solve problems for people, that help to make their lives and environment better, and that contribute to the health and well-being of the nation and perhaps even the world.

When people know that their work is worthwhile and that leaders and organizations are principled and guided by values, values like those that characterize *The Quantum Organization*, they are committed to the work and will do their best to insure that the interests of the company are a priority—that the company's priorities are the individual's priorities as well.

In our team many of us were astounded on a daily basis at the transformation of people from self-centered corporate climbers doing what it takes to get ahead, to owners of the business, holistic business managers always at the ready to improve, support, and lead. This transformation was wholly brought about by living quantum principles.

Setting and Achieving Goals

We became a goal-setting people. We knew that every act, great or small, taken up by men and women began first as a thought, then a goal, and finally action. We remembered again the words of Dr. Dennis R. Deaton:

> We think, and with those thoughts, we create. We create the world we live in...We harvest in life, only and exactly, what we sow in our minds.[8]

We set team goals. We set individual goals. We rehearsed in our minds who we wanted to be, what we wanted to accomplish and how we wanted to achieve our goals. The outcome was startling. We had created a team that was focused and in lock step one with another. It was almost as if conversations between two people instantly propagated throughout the team. There was absolutely no doubt in anyone's mind about what was to be done—the effort was now in creating ways to accomplish the work at hand. If any of you have been in organizations that are not in step and synchronized you know of the vast amounts of wasted time and energy doing rework or hashing out in meetings what to do next. What would you give to have that time and energy returned to you for more productive work?

WHAT ARE THE HARD RETURNS?

Now we are at the part where we get to count the money. As usual it always boils down to money in the end. In business that is as it should be. Businesses are in place to generate revenues, jobs, products, and services, and hopefully to contribute to the greater good of the community, the nation, and the world.

The hard returns derived from the quantum principles outlined in this book can be measured from the perspective of job satisfaction and its correlation to the following components:

1. Customer Retention.
2. Employee Retention.
3. Sales and Profits.
4. Productivity/Accuracy.
5. Absenteeism.

8. Dennis R. Deaton (1996) *The Book on Mind Management,* MMI Publishing, p. 3.

In the beginning establish a baseline of appropriate hard returns, such as sales revenues, customer satisfaction, profits, absenteeism, personnel turnover, and an appropriate measure of productivity for your business (i.e. number of widgets, new product ideas, etc.). To establish your baseline of job satisfaction construct a meaningful survey and ask employees to rate several aspects of job satisfaction on a five-point scale. Ask some open-ended questions to capture the more qualitative aspects of how they feel as well.

If you are attempting to get up-front funding for your quantum reorganization you will have to take some risk and make some predictions regarding ROI and the various hard returns you expect to see. The best approach to establishing expected results is to go with your instincts. You are the best source to evaluate the loss of productivity in your workgroup due to poor job satisfaction. You are also the best one positioned to estimate the benefits of improved morale.

Actual results may vary, but a good rule of thumb is that you can expect at a minimum a 10 percent improvement across the board. In terms of employee retention you can expect very little if any turnover after three months of operating as a true *Quantum Organization.*

The more reliable way is to implement quantum principles in your workgroup and measure actual results. In this way you can establish an accurate and credible comparison between job satisfaction and hard returns and also reduce your risk. The beauty of all this is that in terms of job satisfaction you will see benefits almost immediately. It will take some time to be able to correlate job satisfaction and a hard return on investment (probably six months).

One more thing to keep in mind: quantum principles do not have to be implemented on some broad and expensive scale. You can make a huge difference within very small workgroups. You will be able to make a marked difference in your own satisfaction and self-esteem by adhering to quantum principles as an individual. I guarantee you that once anyone is exposed to quantum principles, even on a small scale, they will want—no demand—more.

Thank you for taking this journey with me. I hope you enjoyed it. Perhaps a small seed of interest has been planted in your heart. As that seed grows you will know with conviction that these are true principles—principles that are meant for us—eternal principles that transcend industry, vocation, avocation, and virtually all of life.

Section 1 Summary

- We must build leadership models based on the principles and the scientific revelations of our time.

- This book was written for those concerned managers who are uneasy with downsizing policies aimed just at boosting stock price.

- In this book you will learn:

  - Effective new leadership tools.
  - How to design effective organizations.
  - How to tap into employees' hidden capacity.
  - How to increase employee productivity.
  - A new and powerful leadership model.

- Opportunities are being lost by not allowing people to bring their whole selves to work.

- The new sciences form the intellectual foundation for many new management concepts:

  - Viewing people in a holistic way.
  - Leadership must be built upon a foundation of relationships.
  - The value of having everyone participate.
  - A more ordered and harmonious workplace.
  - The absolute value of human creativity.

- The unconscious mind is perhaps the last great-untapped resource.

- Our new leadership model is fueled by knowledge.

- Our vision now must include some of these doctrines:

  - The whole really is greater than the sum of the parts—nature is not a machine.
  - Human dialog is critical to creativity. When two ideas that

never met before come together, they lead to or create a new idea.[1]

- As we are all connected to the "cosmic database," it stands to reason that we must organize in a fashion that allows us to tap into this vast array of data.
- Equilibrium is death to *The Quantum Organization.* If human interaction and dialog are critical fuel to the new organization, a little managed chaos thrown into our lives is essential to drive human creativity.
- Complex systems such as organizations are best managed from the bottom up. Today's top-down, command-and-control management styles are complicated, inefficient, and problematic.
- We must manage to recognize the tremendous individual human potential in the workplace. There must be a place at the corporate table for all employees, regardless of physical characteristics, or role or position in the corporate hierarchy.

CHAPTER 2

- People really are a company's greatest asset, its most precious resource.

- Scientists tell us this about the other-than-conscious mind:

  - The subconscious thinks in pictures and images.
  - The subconscious never sleeps.
  - The subconscious mind records everything it sees or hears.
  - The subconscious can be given tasks.

- Feed your personal computer with what it craves—data.

- A key to integrating your message, or your mission, throughout your organization is the creation of new language, new words that evoke an emotional response.

- We must have the courage to go with our instincts, to listen to the still small voice in the back of our mind, to have faith to know that our intuition about these principles is correct while we continue to gain experience and collect the evidence of the truth of this doctrine.

1. For further discussion, see David Bohm (1996) *On Dialogue*, Routledge.

CHAPTER 3

■   Quantum Toolkit includes:

   ■   Dialog.
   ■   Organizational Configurations.
   ■   Self-Forming Teams.
   ■   Information Hub.
   ■   Models as Creative Tools.
   ■   Disequilibrium.
   ■   Quantum Language.
   ■   Strange Attractors.
   ■   Visual Real-time Feedback.

■   Dialog, or the exploration of ideas through dialog, is a foundational characteristic.

■   The four inviolate rules for dialog:

   1.   No criticism of another's ideas is allowed.
   2.   There are to be no winners and losers; simply put, there is to be no debate—when anybody wins we all win.
   3.   Each and every team member must participate—it is the duty of each participant to make sure everyone has a chance to contribute.
   4.   We never leave an idea or a topic unless we are all ready to move on—in dialog there are no agendas.

■   Organizational configurations can and must make sense in fluid networks like *Quantum Organizations*.

■   Some characteristics that every configuration might have:

   ■   Relationships within the networks are key.
   ■   These are learning organizations adaptable to change.
   ■   Ideas are allowed to come forth not by force or hierarchical power, but because they make sense.
   ■   No person or group is independent from the others.
   ■   We have richness as a result of diversity of view and experience.
   ■   The organizational focus is not a matter of who will solve the problem but what wisdom and skill is brought to the table to solve it.

- The old paradigm declares the only way to motivate people is to push them and to prod them; we now know that motivation comes from unrestricted freedom.

- Self-forming teams come into being as need arises to support the work that must get done.

- The information hub has both an informal and a formal nature. The informal component can be the exchanges of thoughts and ideas around the water cooler or the discussions during dialog or those taking place over lunch. The more formal part takes on the look and feel of a board or commission.

- One of the most remarkable and beneficial techniques in our tool-kit is that of the visual model.

- Putting forth ideas, thoughts, principles, and paradoxes is important to creating the instability in the system responsible for initiating change. This is the practice of disequilibrium.

- A few examples of would-be language of *The Quantum Organization*:

  - *Disequilibrium*: the interjection of new information and relationships that challenge the organization; causes the system to reevaluate itself constantly.
  - *Self-organizing*: organizations that evolve and change dynamically to address the needs of the system.
  - *Learning Organizations*: recognition that information is ever changing and that the organization must evolve with the information.
  - *Participative World*: vibrancy of order and accomplishment is a direct result of the numbers and kinds of people who participate in the learning and the doing.
  - *Organizational Intelligence*: recognizing that it is the collective wisdom of the team, not any one person, that brings success and accomplishment.
  - *Strange Attractor*: the few controlling core components of a complex system.
  - *Mind Management*: understanding the full potential of the human mind and then applying it to our life.
  - *Quantum Organization*: the collection of scientific, creative, and intellectual principles that form the foundation of a new leadership paradigm.

- *Pure Knowledge*: the search for all truth and the combination of those truths and our experiences.
- *Dialog*: the act of sharing ideas in a non-confrontational format that encourages discussion of all opinions in order to establish a common content.

- All of the techniques described in this chapter are the product of years of scientific research and countless experiments and trials by error. Each of the tools work—they are all in harmony with the scientific theories that underpin them and they have been shown to be effective in actual practice.

- Visual Real-time Feedback (VRF) creates a tremendous learning experience for both the audience and the presenter. New ideas and concepts are generated and new disciples of the quantum are converted. VRF is a great tool to allow a speaker to interact with a test group to anticipate questions and to prepare and refine his or her delivery to an actual audience.

CHAPTER 4

- The process of synchronizing with nature created great harmony within the workgroup and great confidence within the individual.

- We were all amazed at the increase in the self-confidence of the individual as we were able to express our otherwise submerged thoughts and ideas.

- It is important for team members in *The Quantum Organization* to take full ownership—ownership for their work, their mistakes, their successes, and the well-being of the team and the company.

- The keys to achievement were the tools that allowed the undeveloped thoughts to emerge—without fear of criticism or denigration.

- It was the ability to depend on each other that really fueled our independence. As we were able to rely on the other members of the team to do their part and to do it well, we no longer had to waste time and resources in redundant effort.

CHAPTER 5

- We all have the opportunity to achieve greatness—even if it is only in the eyes of a few, even if we only change the life of the one.

- How do we apply this principle of strange attractor in the workplace–with people?

  - Instead of managing the project we attend to the needs of the people–instead of supervising we lead.
  - Rather than coaching we participate together–we learn from each other.
  - In place of empowering we share power–rather than talking we listen.
  - As an alternative to being served we serve others.

- The most difficult of challenges is the task of overcoming the conventional management wisdom.

- We had five objectives and tactics we used when working with peer groups.

  - It was our objective to educate and inform first, last, and always.
  - We knew that if we could get individuals and teams to participate–to give our concepts a try–we could win them over.
  - Our third objective was to convert people to our view of leadership.
  - We also believed that just like any new doctrine, new converts were going to require ongoing support–support in the sense of retraining, dialog sessions, and political backing.
  - Finally, we knew that we had only scratched the surface in our learning. We wanted to continue to grow intellectually–we wanted to insure that we had a forum for continued exploration of new ideas and the building of a knowledge base that would allow us to challenge the prevailing thinking.

CHAPTER 6

- Value Innovation is a concept based on the notion of rendering the competition irrelevant to your business.

- Most recognized experts in human resource management continue to advocate the classic management and leadership rhetoric that many of us have heard time immemorial. These include the threadbare concepts of:

- Coaching.
- Productive use of strengths.
- Management by objective.
- Process improvement.
- Management by walking around.
- Dress for success.
- Empowerment.
- Total Quality Management.
- Kaizen.
- Measure, analyze, improve, and control.

- Job satisfaction is directly tied to individual self-image and self-esteem.

- The soft returns of our *Quantum Organization* were real, they energized our team, and they provided a spark that ignited a burst of curiosity and creativity throughout the entire organization.

- In *The Quantum Organization* a little planned chaos keeps us on our toes; the hemorrhaging of the best and brightest of our people is devastating.

- What people were experiencing was just right and good; and the loyalty we experienced was a loyalty to ourselves—to our very nature.

- We were really able to glory in the successes of others and sorrow in their losses. Gone was the petty competitiveness that often invades more conventional organizations.

- An important focus of *The Quantum Organization* is the assurance that everyone is engaged in meaningful work—work that contributes towards the shared goals of the team—labor that is challenging and vital.

- The hard returns derived from the quantum principles can be measured from the perspective of job satisfaction and its correlation to the following components:

  - Customer Retention.
  - Employee Retention.
  - Sales and Profits.
  - Productivity/Accuracy.
  - Absenteeism.

The Destination

Introduction

The next several chapters of this book are what set this work apart from others on the topic of leadership and new science—real-life implementation. In this section we will explore the practical implementation of the thoughts, ideas, and theories put forth in the first part of the book. We will explore the actual examples of how we experimented with these new and exciting concepts and found ways to bring them to life in the workplace. This is not to say that there is only one way to make these theories work. On the contrary, by the nature of the quantum world, the world from which these new management ideas were modeled, there is no "one" way—there is no central command, no best practice from which there is no deviation. The beauty of the quantum world is in its somewhat unpredictable nature.

Do not let me scare you off, those of you who revel in the predictable process—in the process that allows no deviation, that insures a certain success and protects from utter failure. I am willing to bet many could give me 100 reasons why the process must be deterministic or predictable to insure results. Well, save the ink. I have heard them all before. In fact, I subscribed to many of them myself—until I saw a better way.

These new techniques will show you how to unleash the power of the human mind—an asset that is absolutely underutilized today in typical business settings.

- We will set the table for a lifelong learning program that will provide fuel to this newly untethered and unencumbered brain that is hungry for information and fresh experiences.
- Next, we will show how organizations can evolve to take advantage of a more unpredictable style and structure. We will offer insights on how individuals must be nurtured and developed through the early stages of organizational change.
- After that we will address the revolutionary changes that must occur to the organization—those things that absolutely must change and change now. These include how we ignite creativity and generate new ideas, how we fundamentally work together, how we manage risk in a more dynamic and somewhat uncertain environment, and more.

- Then we will examine techniques to light the creative inferno that is smoldering within us all. These techniques will include how to tap into the strength of the more creative subconscious mind, the power of pictures and images, and the persuasive influence of language.
- Finally we will solve for S=EPOC, Success=Energy*Passion* Ownership*Creativity. This proven formula will deliver results every time, whether it is at work, at home, or at play.

So please ready your mind and be open to new ideas, a little uncertainty, and an enormous amount of fun. If there is only one point that I make with this book, let it be this: these new theories and techniques will reintroduce fun into your professional vocabulary. The rush of adrenalin present during a creative meeting or gathering is a great ride all by itself. The bonding between people and the thoughts that are shared will reintroduce you to the co-worker that you never really knew—and it will be fun. I promise you that if you give these methods a fair hearing, if you will give them a reasonable try, your life will be changed for the better, and it will be fun.

Chapter 7

Thoughts Have Power

Thoughts have power. Thoughts are energy. You can make your world or break it by your thinking.[1]

THE UNENCUMBERED MIND

There is no greater asset one can bring to a problem than the unen-cumbered mind. Clearing out a mind of its biases, prejudices, and previous leanings is no small task as is obvious to most. We bring with us everywhere we go the personal lenses and filters of our learning and our experiences. For example, for years we have been taught of the value of the top-down hierarchical management structures. Oh yes, we organize and we reorganize, but in the end we still end up with me reporting to you and you reporting to someone else. And this "some-one else" is supposed to insure that we get our work done and get it done right—by the book so to speak. Sometimes we will see the emer-gence of the more enlightened soul that talks about empowering us to get the job done—and other fad management idiom. But in the end, it's me reporting to you and you reporting to someone else.

We have been taught over and over again that to have order we must have people checking on people; without this structure, we will have chaos and inefficiency. It is an old story and further descriptive rhetoric is unnecessary. The point is, this is a given in our lives. We have been taught to believe that without the watchful eye of one of those "someone elses" you and I cannot be trusted to do the right thing—to get the job done efficiently and effectively. If we went onto the street of the average big city in America and asked any ten people we meet, we are likely to get each of the ten telling us the same story: we need that top-down management oversight to insure business succ-ess.

1. Susan Taylor, www.cybernation.com

With this example, we see the effects of a mind that is conditioned to believe that a certain way of looking at a problem is the only way of looking at the problem. Our personal lenses and filters prevent us from opening our minds to myriad possibilities when problem solving or even completing the more mundane daily tasks of the job. It takes great discipline and much practice to remove some of our pre-conditioned responses that we have taken a lifetime to develop. But remove them we must if we are to open our minds to the possibilities of *The Quantum Organization*.

THE POWER OF IMAGES

To limber up the mind and break down some of the old patterns and standards we used pictures and images. We discovered that the old adage "a picture is worth a thousand words" is one of the great understatements of our lifetime. Using pictures, we were able to evoke a tremendous emotional connection between a person and a concept. A real simple example is the powerful image of a New York City firefighter in full gear and smudged face with the American flag as a backdrop. No words are necessary, or in fact able, to communicate the inspiring and patriotic significance of the images of the heroes of 9/11.

A similar impact is felt for the less dramatic messages we want to send in everyday business. We want to create passion and buy-in around vision and mission statements, new business strategies, and even when we are trying to build a little camaraderie within a team. The message here is to build these vision statements with powerful images or pictures, color, and graphics—it communicates so much and creates a lasting image in the mind long after the text has faded.

One of the great sources for powerful and inspiring images comes from the advertising industry. We kept a supply of ad-stock photos and magazine images on hand and used them regularly in meetings, creative sessions, and for use individually. These images were absolutely amazing in their ability to evoke emotion, convey a message, and do so without a word. One of my favorites was a picture of a woman dressed in business attire with a sledgehammer in her hands. She was taking aim at the glass ceiling above her head. Walking on top of the ceiling and in clear view from her vantage point, were the stereotypical male executives dressed in gray suits and totally oblivious to what was happening down below. The expression on the woman's face was priceless—filled with confident determination. No words were necessary, the message was clear. All the history, the struggles, the failures, the successes of the past 25 years of women trying to break into what has been a man's world rush through the mind all at once with perfect clarity, and with powerful focus. It would take volumes of text and months of study to bring a neophyte on par with this issue. Yet it is all made clear with one picture—one image. And what is all the more amazing about images is that their content and meaning is constantly brought to the forefront of the mind by even the briefest exposure to words and language, other images, people, places, and things.

READ THE BEST BOOKS

There are several books that are a must read on the way to reaching a more complete understanding of how the models of the universe can help us manage and run our lives. Though the bibliography at the back of this book gives an extensive reading recommendation, there are four key books that I want to spend some time with here.

Synchronicity

Synchronicity: The Inner Path of Leadership[2] was the first book I read on leadership and the new sciences. It was a good introduction to the notion of a linkage between science and leadership. Jaworski's book is filled with great stories about his life growing up with his famous father (Leon), about his experiences as an attorney, and finally with his quest to understand the synchronous events that seem to be occurring in his life. The book leaves the reader hungering for more solid examples of how the principles uncovered in this book might be better understood and practically implemented. Jaworski does not intend to deliver these pragmatic examples. His goal is to prick our curiosity and entice us to examine the synchronicity in our own lives—to start our own quest for understanding.

Leadership and the New Science

Leadership and the New Science[3] makes a very good effort at encapsulating most of the thinking, phenomena, speculation, and theory on the topic of the sciences and leadership. It causes the reader to contemplate the unique models and patterns that comprise the universe and what a natural matter it is to apply these blueprints and representations to organizations—and really to many aspects of life.

2. Joseph Jaworski (1996) *Synchronicity: The Inner Path of Leadership,* Berrett-Koehler.
3. Margaret J. Wheatley (1999) *Leadership and the New Science,* Berrett-Koehler.

Rewiring the Corporate Brain

Rewiring the Corporate Brain[4] is mostly a comparison between the science of Isaac Newton and the new quantum world discovered by Einstein, Bohr, and others. Zohar does a great job of defining the differences between the old paradigm inspired by the mechanistic perspective of Newton and the new way in which we must think in order to take advantage of our true nature and the true character of the universe in which we live. She goes into some detail describing how the new leadership model would feel, but without descriptions of what it would look like. The book gives us some sense of how we must be flexible and adaptable in order to see how these wonderful and exciting theories can work in the everyday world.

The Six Pillars of Self-Esteem

The Six Pillars of Self-Esteem[5] ranks up at the top of my list of the best and most insightful books I have ever read. Dr. Nathaniel Branden does a superb job of linking achievement to self-esteem and vice versa. Dr. Branden describes self-esteem as "confidence in our ability to think, confidence in our ability to cope with the basic challenges of life." These new models of organization as prescribed by *The Quantum Organization* demand that individuals understand the value of the individual as a cornerstone contributor to the good of the all.

Dr. Branden goes on to tell us self-esteem is "confidence in our right to be successful and happy, the feeling of being worthy, deserving, entitled to assert our needs and wants, achieve our values, and enjoy the fruits of our efforts." One can feel the energy of self-empowerment flowing through the veins while reading that last quote. The Newtonian view subscribes to the notion that what is good for the group is good for the individual. Our intuition whispers to us that this is not true, as evidenced by the record stress-related illnesses in America and the substantial number of diagnosed cases of clinical depression. Our new model tells us something different. It tells us that what is good for the individual is good for the group—not the reverse.

I want to wrap up this section with a plea to embark on a lifelong learning program (we will discuss how in the next chapter). There are many exciting books in publication today that can lay the foundation for learning of leadership and the relationship to science. Start today reading the best books. And who knows, perhaps the book you write may change the world for the better; leaving a lasting legacy for all time.

4. Dana Zohar (1997) *Rewiring the Corporate Brain*, Berrett-Koehler.
5. Nathaniel Branden (1995) *The Six Pillars of Self-Esteem*, Bantam.

ACHIEVEMENT THROUGH SELF-WORTH

To unleash a creative fountainhead requires confidence, poise, self-assurance, and many more similar characteristics—in other words, a positive self-image. Resiliency underpinned by strong self-esteem is absolutely critical in *The Quantum Organization*. Remember, we are challenging the *status quo* like it has never been challenged before. We are hacking away at the cornerstone beliefs that we have grown up with—this will be no easy task. If you really put some thought around what this could be like—taking shots at the corporate sacred cows—you can paint quite a daunting picture. Public humiliations, firings, stalled careers, and so on come to mind first. If this were the 18th century, images of the stocks, dunking, and being burned at the stake would replace our earlier imaginings.

The key to a positive self-image is triggered by real work and real accomplishment. Our experience is clear on this point. While it is always risky to generalize, we found that in the majority of cases when we had problems with an individual's performance the root cause was directly linked to management expectations. Simply put, when an individual had a full job with well-defined rewards and expectations he or she rarely had personal performance issues. On the contrary, the people that were working a full week were in almost all cases the ones generating the new ideas, volunteering for teams and committees, and proactively solving problems. The key was accomplishment. By that I mean that the individuals that had well-defined and reachable goals were our over-achievers. This is not to say that work for work's sake is good. The work has to be meaningful (i.e. have a purpose), the goals must be attainable, and the rewards must be appropriate.

We as individuals know when we are challenged and when we are not. We know when we are working beneath our potential and whether or not we know it; it contributes to our image of ourselves—our self-worth. When a part of the body is damaged or hurt the best medicine is rest—take a load off, so to speak. Not so with our self-esteem. Low self-esteem is put back together not by eliminating work, but by piling on more with difficult but achievable goals, support, and encouragement.

Here are six ways in which you can drive increased productivity by building individual self-esteem through work.

1. Always have meaningful goals. Insure that the goals are measurable, achievable, and have a stretch element.
2. Insure that all work is clearly linked to strategic and operational plans. Each person should know exactly how the work that he or

she is engaged in helps the company achieve its goals.

3. Reward achievement of goals in ways that are meaningful to the individual. Some would consider a lunch or dinner with the Chairman a great treat. Others would count this event as the ultimate torture.

4. Do not allow the poor performance of some workers to destroy the morale and esteem of others. In other words, handle your performance problems swiftly and fairly.

5. Be careful with perks and benefits that further widen the gap between management and staff. By this I mean err on the side of conservatism by limiting if not eliminating huge lavish offices, separate facilities (i.e. dining, lavatory, health) for management and staff, reserved parking, materially better health benefits, and so on.

6. Take joy in the success of others. Give credit where credit is due and for heaven's sake do not take credit for other people's work!

DELIGHT IN THE ACCOMPLISHMENTS OF OTHERS

Critical to staying in harmony with the team and with nature is a pure delight in the accomplishment of others. Encouragement, support, assistance, cooperation, and collaboration are all powerful medicine to the fatigued self-image and fuel to the engaged and impassioned. The act of encouraging others brings to mind the image of the marathon racer rounding the bend for that last mile, no energy left, no zeal for the race—no part of the body that is not screaming out in pain. There to the side of the valiant combatant is an acquaintance, perhaps a coach, maybe just a fan, certainly a friend, running and cheering as if life itself may depend upon the final outcome. It is as if the tired legs and the bone-weary heart have been renewed. The pace picks up, the determined expression on the runner's face reappears, and it is a new race.

It was our experience that the support of the team was a cornerstone to the success of *The Quantum Organization*. Time and time again, as we conducted post mortem reviews of failed or lackluster projects we found that in most cases the failure to achieve the desired results came down to a key leaders' emotional fortitude, or lack of it. By this I mean, when confronted with difficult people, seemingly impossible tasks, and even personal mental fatigue, otherwise good leaders failed to take their performance "up a notch." Simply put, at critical junctures in a project, leaders allowed their self-doubts to undermine the success of the project—rather than push they backed off.

On the other hand, when project leaders had the support of team members—people that were as concerned about the leader's achievement and self-satisfaction as their own—they were successful. There is a great story in nature that has been told over and over again that illustrates this point.

Watch a flock of geese the next opportunity that you have. If you do, what you will see is a near perfect model of teamwork. Each goose flying in "V" formation is part of the greater whole and each knows its role. They take turns flying at the head of the formation where the wind resistance is the greatest and much effort is expended. When a goose tires it falls to the back of the flock and rests. When a goose falls ill or is hurt and must leave the flock another goose follows in support until the ailing goose either recovers or dies. For some time observers have considered the continual honking of the flock as they fly. A bit of an anomaly in nature, this rumpus has mystified researchers. Finally it was discovered what the entire racket means—cheering. The geese are cheering each other on—supporting one another in their common effort.

Recognizing the deeds of others and building excitement within the team for individual and team success delivers huge paybacks. We implemented a five-step program for recognizing and supporting each other:

1. Provide a shadow leader for each person. Sometimes in the legal profession this is called second chair (I know this from watching episodes of *The Practice*—this officially makes me dangerous). The shadow leader provides encouragement, advice and council, and that much-needed emotional support.
2. Understand what kind of recognition the individual desires or responds to. Some respond to monetary rewards and others to personal congratulations while still others enjoy added responsibilities. Remember, what motivates you does not necessarily motivate the next person.
3. Make sure that every person in the organization knows what are the team strategy and goals, and link every piece of work an individual is responsible for to those goals and strategies.
4. Align compensation plans around team goals. The teams must be natural teams with a lot in common. Making everyone part of one great big team is not effective; in fact it is detrimental and drives selfishness and nonconformist behavior.

5. Implement a program to define the key processes in the organization (strange attractors) and to execute on those processes with precision and excellence. This gave us something to cheer about.

Chapter 8

Learning

The only way in which a human being can make some approach to knowing the whole of a subject is by hearing what can be said about it by persons of every variety of opinion and studying all modes in which it can be looked at by every character of mind. No wise man ever acquired his wisdom in any mode but this.[1]

ATTAINING GREAT TREASURES OF KNOWLEDGE

All too often groups, teams, and certainly the individual can get so caught up in the details and volume of the work that they fail to take time, in fact make time to learn and to grow in knowledge. A *Quantum Organization* is a learning organization. The irony of learning is that it is difficult for some people to see the ongoing value of taking the time to grow in knowledge and wisdom, but once an individual or a group catches the spirit of learning this is one element of the organization that becomes indispensable and will take care of itself over time. A simple analogy is the snowball rolling down a snow-covered hill. It takes quite a bit of personal effort and attention to form the ball and push it over and over until it gathers mass and finally has the weight and momentum to propel itself down the hill under its own power. In fact, once the ball of snow gets going it is nearly impossible to stop.

This is not simply about providing training opportunities for people; this is about igniting a passion for learning within the individual— this is not a group exercise. We want those with whom we work (and ourselves, of course) to take personal control of learning. There are not enough training dollars in your budget or free working hours in the day to make learning a top-down exercise. Your challenge is to

1. John Stuart Mill, in Robert L. Heilbroner (1992) *The Worldly Philosophers*, Blackstone Audio Books.

introduce people to the fun and excitement of learning new things—to expanding their field of view. It is your job as a manager to form the snowball and start it on its path, to provide the momentum to start the ball on its journey.

When you see your people being highly selective about what they read, not wanting to waste a moment on mindless or unimportant topics, turning off the television set, excited to share what they have learned, and being selfish about protecting their time for learning you will know that you have succeeded in igniting a passion for learning. These are people that you want to keep around—not only for what they can produce, but also for what they can produce in you.

We will now consider a succinct strategy and action plan for creating an environment of learning.

Put People in Situations where they have to Learn

Several years ago I was leading an effort to redesign the Public Safety division for a large telecommunications company. This division was responsible for maintaining and delivering regional 9-1-1 services for millions of people in the mid-western part of the country. I found myself leading this group purely by chance having no experience, training, or background in the public safety market. I was asked by a good friend to take this division and re-establish it as a top performer from a market perspective, a technology perspective, and to rebuild trust with our customers. What I walked into was a group that had lost its way. This was not just a group that was poorly run or that was underperforming. This was an organization that had lost all contact with the realities of business and customer relationship management. This was a business that needed to be "blown up" and rebuilt from the bottom up.

As I interviewed dozens and dozens of associates and managers of this business I came away with five observations that led to my top priorities:

1. There was very little learning going on with this group. Everyone was stale. There was no reason let alone an opportunity to learn and grow.
2. Management's expectations of employees did not match customer expectations of the company.
3. There was no ownership being taken by management or employees for the success of the business.
4. The lack of leadership towards a clear vision had sapped the energy of the people.

5. In general, the management lacked the business management skills necessary to run this business effectively (or any business for that matter).

I would love to take up your time recounting the myriad experiences that I had with this business division. Fortunately for you and my publisher there is not time enough for that here in this work. However, this experience has been a foundational keystone of my management philosophy and business acumen. What is most important and relevant to the topic at hand is what we all learned addressing number one above: building this group into a learning organization. The simple learning was that when we put people in situations where they had to learn something new we reaped a dramatic reward in terms of organizational wisdom, improved creativity, passion for the work, and the taking of personal ownership for the business.

Having tenured people in jobs certainly has advantages. Knowing how the business runs, who the customer is, how the technology works, and how the business processes work, feels like, and is, a good thing. Having said that, too much time in a job can have disastrous effects on people and on the business. What we found was that too much term in a particular job breeds complacency, a lack of creativity, boredom, and the misguided thinking that there is nothing more to learn.

So we reorganized, we moved people around, we promoted potential, and we removed roadblocks—people and process. The benefits were instantaneous. The energy of the organization was palpable. The organizational learning was:

1. When you place people in situations where they have to learn they do.
2. The act of learning generates energy and passion for the work and for learning itself—learning is contagious.

Simply put, we strategically moved people (starting with managers) into new positions that required them to learn something new in order to meet the requirements of the job. What we observed was a torrent of effort to learn the basics of the new work, creative ways to get the job done, and a renewed passion for the business. It is impossible to measure objectively, but I am convinced that after a matter of a few months the organizational knowledge and wisdom of the business doubled. It showed in our performance both in terms of customer satisfaction and financial returns.

To summarize in a sentence, introducing some calculated and

managed chaos into the business is a key stratagem for a learning organization—for *The Quantum Organization.*

Establish Expectations

Perhaps the most effective tactic for building a learning organization is building expectations of learning. I do not believe that this is a particularly new and radical thought or idea. We have known for centuries that setting goals or establishing expectations is absolutely necessary to achieve an objective. We have known forever that gaining alignment between members of a group in achieving that objective is the essence of success. Nowhere is this clearer than in military operations: Generals establish the objectives and the expectations for taking the hill; Colonels and Majors develop the tactics; and the Captains and the rest take the hill. The important thought here is that as managers of business we must know and believe that a growing, learning organization is core to our success and that we must establish an expectation of learning in our business to be able to reap these important benefits.

In her landmark work *Atlas Shrugged,*[2] Ayn Rand paints a picture of a world (People's States they are called) where, because of the lack of expectations and challenges, most people evolve into unthinking and mindless pawns in a game played by ruthless and selfish leaders against the motive power of men and women. In this philosophical work of fiction Rand creates a stage that allows us to play out the interactions between the prime motivators in human life and the clashes with those thoughts and viewpoints that run counter and fail to motivate.

As depicted in the fictional world created by Ayn Rand, we too play out this fundamental struggle within ourselves to find passion for our work, our play, and our learning. As managers of business we must know that this passion for learning is one of our *strange attractors*[3]— one of the keys we learned about in chapter 1.

Lead by Example

I do not believe there is much left unsaid about the concept of leading by example. Perhaps here I will just issue a reminder.

Leading IS by example.

2. Ayn Rand (1857) *Atlas Shrugged,* Plume.
3. "Strange attractor" is the term scientists have affixed to those few fundamental principles that drive complex systems.

I recall reading about the Confederate charges up Little Round Top at Gettysburg. While these military tactics certainly seem unnecessarily barbaric by 21st century standards, the fact remains that Brigadiers led the charges up the hill into the face of the enemy. It seems to me that having great leaders out in front of the charge is about the only way you could get a person to run into what must have appeared like the jaws of hell. Most of us don't have to face the terrible challenges of warfare, but in our world swimming against the corporate tide can seem a daunting task and one which many of us are unwilling to risk. That is why we need great leaders with vision and with passion about the business, about people, and about getting work done.

Love to Read

I really hope that if you do only one thing I suggest in this book it is that you learn to love to read. Perhaps you already do love to read and if you do you already know the freedom and confidence, the excitement and fun that comes from loving to read. The positive value-add to your self-esteem is almost immeasurable. I think that I learned to love to read about ten years ago. Since that time I have consumed hundreds of books and articles—all of which are neatly stored away in my brain for later use. I love it and I derive great confidence in my work, my relationships, and my life. The one nagging regret that I grapple with from time to time is the wasted years of my life when reading was not central to my day.

The best way to start is to read. Set aside time to read, both on the job and off the job. I use my commute time to listen to audio books. There are great resources for audio books and other good works on tape and CD. I subscribe to an online service that allows me to download audio books to CD or to an MP3 player. It is a great resource for the latest and best books at a great value price. The key to reading is to do it—just do it. Keeping your reading time and the reading time of the people you manage sacred is a must. Make reading a part of your expectations for yourself and your staff.

As important as setting aside proper reading time is selecting the best reading material. Be picky about what you read and be focused in your study. Select topics to study (e.g. marketing, a science, a certain technology, or self-improvement). Set goals for reading, such as to solve a business problem, fix a relationship, or gain a new skill. Having specific goals and working towards those goals is a great motivator and helps one more easily realize the value and benefit of a reading program.

Do it with Questions—Do it with Words

There are two techniques that are quite simple yet almost miraculous in their value and benefit to a learning program:

1. Asking Questions.
2. Writing Answers.

Asking questions in a deep and probing way brings about two benefits. First, it helps the questioner to frame the subject. In other words, it allows the questioner to set the boundaries of the subject. Setting the boundaries of the subject is important, as it tends to expand the topic and allow deeper probing of the subject. As a natural result the expanded probing enlarges the overall learning. Second, asking questions causes the questioned to examine their depth of knowledge on the subject. Deep and probing questioning triggers additional thought and evaluation of the depth to which the topic has been examined, the original premise upon which the answers were based, and the extent to which the topics were researched, and more.

By way of example let's address the value of questioning by examining a sales team in a quarterly operations review. To set the stage, we have a software sales team that has consistently met its sales objectives over the past eight quarters. The team sells into the telecommunications market that has gone through, and is continuing to go through, some significant industry and market turmoil. The sales team feels good about their sales strategy and while their customers are struggling a bit, they have forecasted 7 percent growth in their sales plan for the coming year. The team has delivered to you (the sales manager) an operations plan that provides some detail regarding how they will meet their objectives, who will bring in the revenue, who their customers are, and how they will address each customer (a customer sales strategy).

You have had this document for several days in advance of the review and this has given you plenty of time to review the data and prepare your questions. One thing that strikes you is that this review looks pretty much the same as the past several reviews in terms of customer and sales strategy, even though the industry is changing and uncertain. You know that joblessness and earnings in the telecom market space are continuing to worsen. The world is much more unstable, making global expansion somewhat problematic. You have seen a marked change in the way people spend in the United States as a result of the tragedy of 9/11. There is a growing demand for public safety applications that clearly must be delivered by newer and more robust telecommunications infrastructure. There has been a change in the political climate of the country after the November 2002 elections. Republican control of the Senate, the House of Representatives, and the White House may bring about some material changes to the telecommunications act of 1996 and at the Federal Communications Commission (FCC) that controls much of the telecommunications in the country. The head of the FCC, Michael Powell, is the son of the current Secretary of State in this Republican-dominated administration.

So you sit with your team and you probe their thinking and the basis for their plan and strategy. You ask: why did you do that, why do you think that will work, how are you going make that happen, what are you going to do if your plan does not produce results, who is going to do that, does he or she have the skills necessary to be successful? You ask if they have considered this or have they considered that. You may find that they have thought through many of the market dynamics of the telecommunications industry. However, you may also find that they have not changed the market plan and their business model for two years: it has been successful up until now—why tinker with a good thing? In any event, what you have done is you have challenged their thinking and expanded their scope. As a good manager you will send them back to do additional research and to explore a new and different approach to the market. They may come back with the same plan or something similar, but you now know that they have thought this out much more thoroughly and expanded their knowledge. By asking probing questions you not only learn for yourself but you cause your people to take a deeper dive into the business and think through their decisions. You may ask them to go back and model the industry using the techniques we talked about in chapter 3.

Asking deep and probing questions is a critical tool for a manager in *The Quantum Organization*. Do you remember the questions posed in the Introduction of this book?

- Where is the energy?
- Why is there no passion for the work evident when two or more people gather in the name of the company?
- You may even ask yourself who is leading this bunch—who is taking ownership to insure an atmosphere of energy, passion, and creativity?

Complacency and the sense of being satisfied have no place in *The Quantum Organization*. Asking questions and challenging the thinking of people is a simple and most effective way to keep your team creative and sharp—to keep yourself sharp.

Asking questions and writing answers are Siamese twins in *The Quantum Organization*. There is nothing that will add more to the deep and clear understanding of a topic than to write about it—nothing more valuable. When we are exploring a new topic and beginning the cognitive evaluation of the associated data and information, our mind tends to be able to mix in together well-thought-out ideas and those concepts that are still undeveloped or "fuzzy." Often times we tend to think that we have made a fairly complete examination of all aspects of this new idea. Upon closer inspection (through questioning perhaps) we discover that our thinking is not complete at all. Those fuzzy thoughts are just that—fuzzy. Write it down—develop a white paper, write yourself a memo, write a book—but write it down. It is nearly impossible to write down undeveloped or unclear thoughts without it becoming crystal clear that more work is needed to complete the thinking.

I could fill this book with the stories of the countless times that through deep and probing questioning followed up with a written thesis on the subject I have experienced the power of this invaluable learning technique. As I have stated before, the concepts of *The Quantum Organization* are new and they go against the traditional wisdom of our age. You must read, ask questions—lots of questions, and write about what you think you know. For me personally, this book has been the ultimate exclamation point and tribute to this thought. As I wrote the outline for *The Quantum Advantage* I was sure that I had researched, tested, and experienced all that was necessary to complete this book. It was only through the actual writing that I discovered the depth of knowledge that I possessed or needed to possess to cover these topics appropriately. What a fabulously fulfilling and valuable experience this has been for me—I recommend it highly to you.

TAPPING INTO THE COLLECTIVE WISDOM OF THE GROUP

Another vital step in establishing *The Quantum Organization* is the notion of tapping into the collective wisdom of the group, nature, and the universe. Spending time together and reasoning out solutions to problems, engaging in the creative process, and simply engaging in free-form discussion is a cornerstone characteristic of *The Quantum Organization*. What rich and rewarding experience these moments of sharing are. When the group comes together with that breakthrough idea or that long-awaited epiphany it is a learning experience beyond compare. In this section we will give a practice for organizing such interactions while still being able to get the day's work done.

There are two keys to tapping into the intelligence and knowledge of the group:

1. Finding and taking the time to dialog.
2. Structuring that time together.

Finding the Time to Dialog

Carving out the time to spend in dialog with your team might be one of your most difficult challenges. If your workplace is like most, the "fire-fighting" tends to overtake the planned events. Dialog is absolutely one aspect of *The Quantum Organization* that you must not let fall to the bottom of the priority list. One way to make sure you have time for creative dialog is to redefine the time you spend together today. This means that you do not necessarily have to create more time together, but you simply spend the time you are together in a different way—you make all your time together with your teams "dialog time."

Let me give a related example of what I mean by redefining your time together. One of the more rewarding jobs I held during my career in the telecommunications business was leading the 2002 Olympic Winter Games sponsorship for my company. On 8 September 1997 it was announced that US WEST (now Qwest) would be a major sponsor of the Olympic Winter Games in Salt Lake City, Utah, in 2002. The sponsorship began 1 April 1998 and included sponsoring the US Olympic teams in 2000 to Sydney, Australia, and 2004 to Athens, Greece. Other telecommunications companies such as Lucent Technologies, AT&T, and Samsung would also provide products and services to the Games. As you would expect, telecommunications plays a critical role in making the Games a global event.

This global event is an opportunity for companies like US WEST and Lucent to demonstrate to the world that their products and services are superior and that their employees are the best in the world at delivering those products and services. However, this will not happen without a focused strategy across all their lines of business and a powerful marketing plan executed with precision. This will happen as a result of overarching programs that provide for the needs of all business units and other departmental organizations. These programs will provide a set of integrated tools, programs, promotions, and opportunities intended to support and compliment the other activities that take place on a day-to-day basis across the company.

With that as a background it does not take much more imagination to realize that an Olympic sponsorship is a huge undertaking. It will take time—lots of time, people—lots of people, and money—lots of money. Or does it? A strategy that we employed to help us keep a line on costs was something we called "Olympisizing." It is a simple yet potent device that allowed us to keep costs to a minimum while still meeting the huge and growing needs of an Olympic sponsorship. Simply put, we tagged the advertising that we were already doing with the Olympic rings and logos, we took the employee and customer rewards programs that were in place and gave them an Olympic theme, and we took the network construction programs that were already planned and tweaked them to meet the needs of the Games—we "Olympisized" our normal operations.

Again, this means that you do not necessarily have to create more time together (though spending more time together is OK), but you simply spend the time that you are together in a different way—you make all your time together with your teams "dialog time."

If you recall from chapter 3 we had some rules for engaging in dialog:

1. No criticism of another's ideas is allowed.
2. There are to be no winners and losers, simply put, there is to be no debate—when anybody wins we all win.
3. Each and every team member must participate—it is the duty of each participant to make sure everyone has a chance to contribute.
4. We never leave an idea or a topic unless we are all ready to move on—in dialog there are no agendas.

As a first step, take these rules and apply them to the meetings that you already have with your teams and with other groups you meet within the normal course of your business day. Bear in mind that while accomplishing tasks is an important part of meetings, tapping into the collective wisdom of the groups has to be the centerpiece objective for meeting together—for it is through sustained thinking and the application of knowledge that we accomplish work. Next, we will discuss the structure of a meeting based on dialog.

Structured Dialog

So now we have a strategy for spending quality time together with our teams and co-workers. Structuring that time for the best results is next. That said it is heresy to use the words structure and dialog in the same sentence in my opinion. The nature of dialog is unstructured. It is from this unstructured quality that we are able to tap into the hidden knowledge that exists within us all. While structure and agendas tend to be the enemies of dialog, creating an environment that is conducive to good dialog takes some effort and forethought. Here is a bulleted list of some actions or steps that can lead to a fertile atmosphere for dialog:

1. Spend time teaching your teams what dialog is (and is not).
2. Post the rules for engaging in dialog in your meeting rooms and offices.
3. Aggressively follow the rules for dialog.
4. As a leader/manager remember that your voice is simply one of many with equal weight—act accordingly.
5. Allow others to facilitate meetings—use pop-up leadership (see chapter 3—Self-forming Teams).
6. Use the techniques described in chapter 3 to stimulate creativity.
7. Draw out the quiet people.
8. Follow a discussion thread until discussion around this thread has been exhausted regardless of the tangents you may go down (see rule 4).
9. Do not watch the clock. If you have to extend the meeting time or reconvene another meeting then do so. Remember, the objective is to tap into the knowledge and wisdom of the group, not meet timelines.
10. Encourage each other (see rule 1).

Take good notes and enjoy the increased flow of information, the new creative ideas, and watch the relationships and bonds between people grow.

LISTENING TO THE STILL-SMALL VOICE

Let's talk about that still-small voice that we sometimes refer to as our inner-self, our instincts, or our gut feelings. I am not going to offer any great insights to this voice of reason—this personal guide. I will touch on what it might be and then I am going to make a case for listening to it as a learning tool. So what are some of the possible sources of this still small voice?

- The soul or the sprit.
- Our subconscious mind.
- The Cosmic Database—fields of energy.

- A higher intelligence or being.
- Some combination of the above.

I am not sure it really matters what is the source of this terrific companion or voice that is with us constantly. What matters is that we tap into this flow of knowledge and insight that is literally at our fingertips twenty-four hours a day, seven days a week. My personal experience and the outcome of the research we conducted putting into practice the concepts of *The Quantum Organization* tells me that regardless of its source, the still-small voice is a real source of knowledge, insight, and power.

If this voice is our spirit or soul speaking to us from eons of existence and experience then we should listen and act. If the source were some higher intelligence or being guiding our path then we would be fools to ignore it. Or if somehow our subconscious mind is able to tap into the quantum nature of the universe and gain access to a vast history of knowledge and information then all the better that we learn to control it and tap into this knowledge and use it to our advantage. Perhaps it is just our subconscious mind working on the problems that we put to it, using the information that is stored in our brains from a lifetime of learning. Regardless, we have all felt its presence, we have followed the voice to our success and we have all ignored it to our detriment and missed opportunity.

Whatever the source for this voice we must learn to listen to it. I personally practice listening to this voice in several ways, one of which is through meditation and thought. I spend at least one hour per day, and not all at once, practicing listening to this voice—my companion. I find a quiet place where I can be comfortable and I just listen and I learn. Sometimes it is in my car, in my office, or at home. Often times I begin by reading a good book or I put on soothing music and I let my mind wander and I listen. Another powerful way I listen is I obey. For example, when driving my car, if I get that feeling to stop and pull over, change my course home after a busy day, or to slow down and change lanes, then I do it. I have never avoided a bad car wreck (at least to my knowledge) or found some pot of gold on the side of the road, but I still obey. This practice helps me to keep my mind focused and listening. Another great example that has delivered real tangible results is in my relationships. When that voice warns me not so say those words that I know I will regret, I follow the advice, I learn, and I benefit. But on those countless times when I do not listen and say things that cannot be taken back or undone—and saying "I am sorry" just doesn't make it alright—I chastise myself for not listening and I vow to be better and follow the voice.

The concepts of this thing we are calling *The Quantum Organization* are new and as with anything new and out of the ordinary it will take time and some sacrifice to bring these ideas into the mainstream. But as with everything in life it starts with thought and then one man or woman putting that thought into action. It starts with you, here and now—no one is coming to do this for you. You can make a difference one day at a time and one person at a time.

Chapter 9

Evolving Existing Organizations

Whatever relationships you have attracted in your life at this moment, are precisely the ones you need in your life at this moment. There is a hidden meaning behind all events, and this hidden meaning is serving your own evolution.[1]

WORKING IN THE SYSTEM

S ome characteristics of *The Quantum Organization* are better accomplished through evolution. In most cases, much of what is going on in your business is good and should be retained and tweaked. Building *The Quantum Organization* is as much about evolution as it is about revolution—sometimes you must eat the elephant one bite at a time. It is a process of changing policies and working within the system (i.e. internal political systems and corporate cultures).

Think of this evolution like training for a marathon. There are many things to address when preparing for a 26-plus mile road race. Your back must be straight and upright and slightly leaning forward, your arms bent at the elbow, swaying back and forth with the motion of your body. You should have your shoulders low and loose—not tense, and you should keep your head straight, following the same lean as your back. There are slight adjustments for your mouth and lips, your hands, and even your thumbs. There are training tips and nutritional changes to your daily intake of food and so on. Preparing for a race like a marathon is a big change in one's life. Yet it is not about revolution, it is about evolution—slight changes to posture, adjustments to nutrition, and improved and focused exercise routines.

Perhaps you are thinking, "Stop! I mean what is this *thumbs here* and *lips there*? We all know how to run: you pick up your feet and quickly place one foot down in front of the other and you don't stop

---

1. Deepak Chopra (2000) *The Conscious Universe*, Hay House Audio.

until you reach the finish line." I learned this as a kid and have not forgotten how to do it even today. Alas, unlearning what we have learned at the hands of well-meaning but unenlightened teachers and role models is problematic in most of what we do in life—certainly it is true in building *The Quantum Organization*. Truth be told, these slight corrections to our running style are absolutely critical to running a good and efficient race. The same is true as we make adjustments in how we learn, how we interact with people, and how we implement these new quantum changes in our work, our homes, and at play. The impacts of change on the organization are new and will be difficult to get our minds around at first. Our goal is an evolutionary change away from the top-down command-and-control organization, so prevalent in today's workplace, to a more level-less quantum model.

Planting Seeds

Planting seeds is one technique that is invaluable in beginning the evolution to a more quantum-like model. Often times I find myself between two dilemmas when I am faced with making necessary changes within an organization. Do I, after careful evaluation, introduce top-down changes or commands to process and organization, or do I work in a more evolutionary fashion by planting the seeds of change and watching them germinate and grow? In the next chapter we will address the revolutionary changes—in this chapter we will plant the seeds of change, nurture them, and watch them grow.

While working for a smaller software and data transaction delivery company I found it necessary to make some significant changes to some key processes and to the culture itself. This is and was a very good company and by far the extent of its problems stemmed from the issues surrounding a great little company experiencing some significant growth through market expansion and acquisition. Needless to say, the difficulties are obvious to anyone that has worked in such an environment:

- Smaller companies can have a tendency to rely on the heroics of a few to pull their fat off the fire when problems arise instead of good solid repeatable process.
- Smaller companies, particularly technology companies, tend to put a higher premium on tactics instead of strategy. Simply put, some smaller companies have not needed to understand the finer points of laying out technology and market strategies and then building tactics to address and reach those strategic goals.

■ Some smaller companies tend not to be as focused on customers as on their product.

These three generalizations of small companies instead of large companies are certainly debatable regarding their application in one small company vs another. I mention them because they were prevalent in the company I worked for, they do tend to be true in a portion of small companies, and they pretty much represent my experience, though your experience may be different.

In any event, my company was experiencing some growing pains and during the last half of 2002 the pain was getting particularly acute. Our software contracts with our customers called for us to deliver two major update releases of our code each year. We staffed our software development team accordingly—to meet the terms and conditions of our contracts. In 2002 alone we delivered more than eleven different major loads or releases of software, all of which missed their promised delivery date and all of which ended up going out of our doors with major problems (or "bugs" in the industry vernacular). To give credit where credit is due we did not knowingly send out any code with severe problems, but these problems raised their ugly heads when the customer ran the software into their test cycles. So not only was the software initially delivered late but as a result of the bugs in the software the customer had to stop testing in most cases and wait for us to fix the problem and send them an update in order for them to continue with their testing. This impacted their test schedules, their ability to put the software into live production, and it impacted their availability to schedule test and production resources (people) and increased their overall costs—needless to say they were a bit testy with us.

The root causes of this problem were many. Three of the key contributors were:

1. We were putting out too many releases of our software compared to our staffing levels—eleven in 2002 vs staffing for two.
2. We were being too accommodating of our customers in terms of agreeing to additional releases (that was due to the hero in us).
3. We were not allowing ourselves enough time to test the software adequately.

As I contemplated a strategy to get this group back on track and producing the quality product that they were capable of, it occurred to me that this was an ideal opportunity to put into practice some quantum processes and tools. This would be the first time that this group would be exposed to quantum tools and practices. I decided to introduce these tools surreptitiously into the daily routine of meetings and conference calls—all of the normal interactions between teams and team members. I started with dialog. Remember, at this point in the problem-solving process we had not as yet identified the root causes of the problem.

In one particular group meeting, we were experiencing some inconsistency in our communications with our customer over more rounds of late product deliveries. We quickly formed a team to investigate the problem and develop a resolution—a comprehensive communications strategy and plan. I mapped out a few meeting strategies:

1. As the organizational leader of the team I wanted to resist the urge to take control of the meeting and establish myself as the focal point of discussion. I would allow and encourage pop-up leaders to emerge.
2. I would use silence (*my* silence) as a tool to encourage participation.
3. I would have no agenda.
4. I would assume the responsibility of ensuring a balanced participation between all participants.
5. I would enforce the no-debate—only dialog rule.

The results were fabulous. This group of people was hungry for the chance to work the problem as a team. These professionals were, whether they knew it or not, looking for a forum to sit and discuss the problems we all knew were eating us alive in the market and damaging our credibility with our customers. The right forum and the right process unleashed a wave of creativity that quickly brought us to recognition of the root causes and resolution to the problem.

This team had spent no time in training with any of the quantum thoughts or theories. No one knew what I was doing let alone what I had planed for them with this meeting strategy. It was as if this new approach to problem solving was simply in their nature. Sure, it took a few uneasy moments for the team to get in the spirit of it all. I am sure that many were confused by my silence and by the role that I assumed as the meeting got into gear. However, no one was displeased with the outcome—no one could deny the energy and passion in the room.

If I have given you the impression that building towards *The Quantum Organization* is all about revolution, then I must stop you here and clear up this matter. *The Quantum Organization* is about getting in touch with our true nature and organizing and executing our work in harmony with that nature.

It is like the difference between swimming upstream and swimming downstream, running uphill and running downhill; it is about the tweaks and twists, and the tugs and pulls on how we do things today— it is a little oil here and a little oil there. Your teams will recognize a good thing when they see it (and feel it). Quantum techniques will catch hold a lot quicker with your teams if they experience it first hand for themselves. Besides, it takes a lot of personal energy, probably more than you have, to introduce a new system with no support, no process, and no executive sponsor. Start small and be patient—it will be worth it.

GIVING EACH PERSON MEANINGFUL WORK

Each person needs meaningful work. An individual must feel that they are an important part of the team. They also must know how the work that they do contributes to the overall success of the corporation and the benefit of the community. We conducted several focus group sessions with typical employees from all ranks and files. We put to the groups this question: How important is it that you understand how the work you do will contribute to the strategic direction of the company? Below are some of the verbatim answers to this question:

"...It is impossible for me to make good informed decisions within the scope of my job unless I know what is important to the company."

"...It frustrates me to no end when I work my tail off trying to meet a customer's need or working to drive new business only to find out that what I have delivered is not in the plan."

"...How am I expected to know the direction of the company if no one takes the time to tell me, or if no one thinks it is important that I know?"

"...Lacking any other direction, I will do my job the best I can according to what is important to me!"

"...When I am left out of the information loop it sends a very clear message to me regarding my priority and standing in the company..."

"...When I am not given the necessary information that I need to do my job it tells me something about the people I work for."

"...It is beyond me how these managers can be successful in their personal lives with such behavior. No one would agree that nurturing personal relationships, or raising children, or dealing with the person at the Dry Cleaners can be done with any degree of success when we don't communicate."

"...Someone is asleep at the switch. That is a heluvaway to run a railroad."

It does not take a whole lot of additional insight to draw up a pretty sobering list of the problems managers face when they do not communicate direction and the importance and value of the work their teams are doing.

1. Lack of alignment leads to inefficiencies and increased costs.
2. Unrest and frustration causing loyalty, employee turnover, and other retention issues.
3. Lack of confidence in management leads to poor morale and other leadership shortfalls.
4. Lack of appropriate focus on corporate direction causes missed sales opportunities and a variety of customer relationship losses.
5. The loss of employee productivity could be as high as 30 percent[2] when comparing the output of an employee that is in full alignment with the corporate objectives and has a passion for the work he or she is engaged in.

If you ever have the chance to spend some time with people that work in the Public Safety industry I recommend that you have a discussion about passion in the workplace for the job. I have had the distinct pleasure of working in the emergency 9-1-1 industry over the years where it is easy to find people with passion for the work that they do.

I first encountered this phenomenon when I was asked to lead the Public Safety group for my company in 1996 (I introduced you to this company at some length in chapter 8). While this group clearly had some problems, most of which stemmed from poor management, one shining star was the passion the people had for their work. In the time that I spent with this team I discovered that almost to the person (I believe that most people in the group were passionate about this business, but there were some that I was never 100 percent certain about) these people loved their job, identified with the work, and were proud to tell their friends that they worked for and with the delivery of 9-1-1 service. These people were not working with data and communications networks, they were saving lives.

It was here that I first saw the absolute undisputable powers of having a focused and passionate team working in total alignment towards

2. See chapter 1 overview, see Guthrie and Cascio studies.

a common vision. When we were able to get management out of the way this team performed; it seemed to gain energy as the day progressed, and productivity soared.

Here are some tips that will help you insure that you are giving meaningful work to your teams:

- Spend time clearly articulating your strategy (including missions and visions).
- As you *operationalize* these strategies make sure that you address how the work of each person in your organization is aligned with and helps support the strategy.
- Talk to your people in terms of how the work you do or the products that you make help people, support the environment, save time and money, and so on.
- Redefine the business you are in, from the products that you make to the things that the products you make do for people. As in our earlier example, this is the business of saving lives, not just managing data and delivering telecommunications services.
- Engage in both a top-down and a bottom-up communications plan that insures people have the information they need and that you have the information that only your teams have. Watch for information roadblocks at the middle layer of your management team. Make sure that you are not an information roadblock.
- Use quantum tools (see chapter 3) to unleash the creativity of your organization.
- Move with method as you introduce these recommendations into your business. Remember this is about evolution and not revolution. Give people time to be passionate about their work. Let them decide what to be passionate about. Create a fertile environment and plant some seeds.

INSURING THE HEALTH AND WELL-BEING OF PEOPLE

The health and personal well-being of the individual is important to *The Quantum Organization*. Stress is a contributing factor in heart-related deaths in the country. A major cause of stress is our occupations—our jobs. It then stands to reason that mounting stress must contribute to a degradation of performance over time. Doctors tell us that:

> Heart patients can dramatically lower their chance of having more cardiac problems by utilizing stress-reduction techniques, according to the results of a new study reported in the American Medical

Association's Archives of Internal Medicine. Researchers at Duke University took 107 heart patients and put them on either a four-month stress-reduction program, a four-month exercise regimen or allowed them to receive usual heart care from their personal physicians. Only three of the 33 people given stress management suffered cardiac events, defined as a heart attack or heart surgery such as a bypass or angioplasty.[3]

We also know what causes stress-related damage to our bodies (besides the boss on a Friday at 3:00 asking for that 40-page report by the close of business). Here is the condensed version. When we are under stress our bodies produce larger than normal quantities of insulin. The body converts insulin into glycogen that our muscles use for energy. Our bodies are gearing up for what is commonly known as "fight or flight." This is easy to see if we use the example of a person suddenly encountering a bear while hiking in the woods—clearly a stressful situation by anyone's standards. We have two obvious choices—fight the bear or run for our life. Fortunately, our body understands our needs in this kind of situation and it provides us some additional fuel to support our choice. We are creating a store of quick energy in order for us to exert some physical energy to combat our enemies. The problem is that this is all well and good if you are faced with a bear in the forest, but in the office our over abundance of glycogen usually has no attendant physical energy to burn this fuel. The good thing about glycogen is it provides us much-needed energy. The bad news is that too much unburned glycogen will begin to attack and destroy our internal organs—this is how stress kills.

What all this amounts to is that the health and well-being of employees has a direct bearing on the costs of doing business. Business has known this for some time now as we have been encouraging exercise, providing health-care benefits, and as of late supporting wellness benefits for employees. Building employee health and wellness programs will take constant attention over time.

Twenty years ago it was heresy to suggest that corporations spend money and time on building health facilities at work locations or to subsidize worker fees at the local gym—even today, in some companies it is still heresy. However, the trend is changing. Gyms and workout facilities are popping up all over corporate America. It has taken time but senior management is finally getting the message about the linkage between the health of employees and productivity.

In the end, there are huge changes that must be made in order to

3. CNN Plus article, "Stress Management Reduces Heart Attack Risk", October 1997, http://www.cnn.com/HEALTH/9710/19/heart.stress/

transform the traditional organizational structures and corporate management policies from a mechanistic and command-and-control configuration into a make-up based on our quantum nature. Some of these changes are going to take some time and they must evolve much as the sluggish and nondescript caterpillar changes into the swift and stunning butterfly. It is a change, a metamorphosis, from the tired and well-worn practices of the past to the new and more freethinking ideas we discussed in Section I of this book. This transformation is really a lifelong journey as much as it is a revolutionary redesign of all that we have come to know as management.

Chapter 10

Organizational Revolution

Boundaries? What boundaries? [1]

INTRODUCTION

Some characteristics of *The Quantum Organization* are better accomplished through revolution. In many cases, much of what is going on in your business is not good and should be immediately restructured. Building *The Quantum Organization* is as much about revolution as it is about evolution—sometimes you must eat the elephant in one bite. It is a process of redefining the way we think and undoing centuries of training and misinformation.

In the American Revolution we find an analogy for the changes we must make in how we manage people—in how we manage our business—it is truly a revolution.

> General Thomas Gage, an amiable English gentleman with an American-born wife, commanded the garrison at Boston, where political activity had almost wholly replaced trade. Gage's main duty in the colonies had been to enforce the Coercive Acts. When news reached him that the Massachusetts colonists were collecting powder and military stores at the town of Concord, 32 kilometers away, Gage sent a strong detail from the garrison to confiscate these munitions.
>
> After a night of marching, the British troops reached the village of Lexington on April 19, 1775, and saw a grim band of 70 Minutemen—so named because they were said to be ready to fight in a minute—through the early morning mist. The Minutemen intended only a silent protest, but Major John Pitcairn, the leader of the British troops, yelled, "Disperse, you damned rebels! You dogs, run!" The leader of the Minutemen, Captain John Parker, told his troops not to fire unless fired at first. The Americans were withdrawing when someone fired a shot, which led the British troops to fire at the Minutemen. The British then charged with bayonets, leaving eight dead and ten wounded. It was, in

---

1. Angelina Georgescio, www.houseofquotes.com

the often quoted phrase of Ralph Waldo Emerson, "the shot heard 'round the world."[2]

We too must fire our own shot to be heard around the world. Certainly our shot will not take the form of lead and gunpowder, but it will be as spectacular and just as revolutionary as that dramatic moment at Concord. Lives may not be at stake, but life and our self-esteem unquestionably is. Our nemesis may not be as obvious and palpable, but it is nonetheless as real. Our challenge is to undo the ruinous management practices and policies that have been crafted for us beginning in the days of Sir Isaac Newton and in the days of the Industrial Revolution, and raised to an art form with the 1950s management practices that we are saddled with today. This mechanistic view of humankind fails to deliver on the full potential of people. It fails to coexist peacefully with the true nature of our humanness.

It is time to make a few changes. It is time to change dramatically some of our most sacred fundamentals that have been cornerstones to our management philosophy of the past 100-plus years:

1. Top down command-and-control management and complex hierarchical organization structures are inefficient and are roadblocks to human creativity—they must go and go now.
2. Not only is the command-and-control management practice inefficient, it absolutely stifles human growth—men and women grow and increase only through their own agency.
3. Machine-like assembly-line operations are the kiss-of-death to growth and learning—the introduction of a little managed chaos into an organization is absolutely necessary.
4. Managing complex systems starts from the bottom up and not from the top down—strange attractors are the key to managing complex systems.
5. Debate and other competitive techniques for drawing out and exploring new ideas clearly stand in the way of personal expression and idea generation—it is time for dialog to replace debate.

SELF-FORMING TEAMS IN ACTION

As we discussed in chapter 3, self-forming teams come into being as need arises to support the work that must get done. Creating *The Quantum Organization* is a process of building and applying relation-

2. *An Outline of American History,* 1994, chapter 3, "The Revolution Begins",
   http://odur.let.rug.nl/~usa/H/1994/ch3_p8.htm

ships and not one of a specific hierarchy. We bring people together, the people with the appropriate skills, in a very dynamic fashion to solve problems and get work done.

Let's face it and face it now—those of us in control like it and don't want to give it up. Hey, it is comfortable and if we are honest with ourselves—we like it. It gives us a sense of dominion. History is rife with examples of what the desire for power can do—it can be a great motivator. We get not a few entries in our dictionaries and books of language as a result of this unquelled thirst for power as well:

- Despot.
- Dictator.
- Tyrant.
- Autocrat.
- Oppressor.
- Authoritarian.

History also gives us plenty of examples of teams and individuals working together towards a common goal; each understanding his or her own role, each sharing a part of a vision, and each reveling in the success of the individual and the team—each rising to the task as events unfold.

One such example is the monumental task of the building of the transcontinental railroad in the 1860s in North America. To this day we must stand in awe of the accomplishment. It is all the more spellbinding when we consider that it was essentially done without the aid of much technology—no cars, trucks, pneumatic drills, or tractors—no modern motive power at all other than the steam-powered train itself, and that only really usable after the track was built. Millions of tons of rails and equipment had to come from the east to the west via sailing ships around Cape Horn after months'-long journeys fraught with peril and danger. Many ships and their precious cargo were lost and still rest at the bottom of dark and icy seas. Many workers lost their lives as a result of accidents, bitter cold, other violence, and even the odd Indian raid. The Central Pacific railroad (beginning in the west and building eastward) and the Union Pacific (working from east to west) employed thousands upon thousands of men and women in this great effort. They met the challenge of the severest of mountain peaks, dry and unforgiving deserts, and some of the most brutal snowstorms and perilous weather in recorded history.

Our task may not seem as momentous as the building of the largest railroad in the world, but we have our challenges as well—we too have our Rocky Mountains. At times it may even seem that the building of a railroad doesn't seem like so difficult a task—you grade the road, you lay the ties, and you drop and spike the rails. The task is clear, the endpoint is obvious, and everybody knows his or her job. Not necessarily so these days. The nature of what we do today may not be as physically challenging as building a railroad in 1867, but the complexity will kill you.

It is the complexity that demands that we manage our work and ourselves in different ways. Do you recall the analogy of the tree and its roots given earlier in the book? Trying to manage the individual growth of each leaf is impossible, but if you nurture and care for the roots the leaves will take care of themselves.

One such root is a self-forming team. Self-forming teams need these five things in order to take root and grow:

1. A clearly developed problem statement or goal.
2. Well-communicated and understood ground rules for the teams.
3. Team members with the ability to thrive in unstructured organizational environments.
4. Patient and supportive management.
5. Measurements of success.

Problem Statements

When teams have a clear understanding of where they are headed in almost all cases you can count on achieving the desired outcome. In the more unstructured setting of the self-forming team it is absolutely necessary to have clearly articulated goals or you can always count on missing your target. Pop-up leadership can only happen as a by-product of dialog around the problem statement.

Ground Rules

The ground rules for self-forming teams are:

- Anyone can lead the team.
- There is no voting for team leadership.
- A leader will emerge through the normal course of dialog and discussion of the problem statement.
- Be patient—let nature take its course.
- Take courage—when it feels right to take charge then have the courage to step-up and lead the team.

Less Structured Organizations

Unstructured or less structured organization does not equate to chaotic, unmanaged clatter. Unstructured in this case means fluidly structured or virtually structured. It means that team leadership should be a product of having the right people step-up and lead according to the problem and the required skills to achieve the goal. Once the team forms, normal guidelines for managing projects and conducting meetings apply—be on time, respect others, complete your assignments, establish measurements of success, and so on.

Patience

Allowing teams to form appropriately may take only a few minutes of the first team meeting; it may also take more than one discussion session to delve deeply enough into the problem to understand enough about root causes and what needs to be done—all of which must be explored at length to allow the teams to form. Be patient, especially at first. Keep the dialog robust and vigorous and the teams will form.

Measurements

One of the first things that the team leader needs to establish is the indicator that demonstrates that the problem has been solved or the goal has been reached. Book upon book has been written extolling the value of establishing metrics and measuring progress towards goals. We will not tarry longer on this topic here other than to say do not forget this oft overlooked and yet critical aspect of team management.[3]

FREE AGENCY—A CATALYST FOR PERSONAL GROWTH

Free agency is as much about the process of choosing as it is about the fact that we get to choose.

What most scholars agree upon that sets human beings apart from the animal world is our freedom of choice; the freedom to choose our way sans any pre-programmed instincts or impulse. Of course, in order to

3. Some additional reading on the topic of problem solving, process/self-improvement, and metrics include: Gary Hamel (2002) *Leading the Revolution*, Plume; Goldratt and Cox (1982) *The Goal: A Process of Ongoing Improvement*, North River Press; Harry and Schroeder (1999) *Six Sigma: The Breakthrough Management Strategy Revolutionizing the World's Top Corporations*, Doubleday; Mager and Pipe (1997) *Analyzing Performance Problems*, CEP; Stephen R. Covey (1990) *The 7 Habits of Highly Effective People*, Simon and Schuster; Wayne F. Casico (2002) *Responsible Restructuring*, Berrett-Koehler.

exercise this gift, beings must have more than a rudimentary cognitive capability—which we do.

In chapter 7 we said this about our self-esteem:

The key to a positive self-image is triggered by real work and real accomplishment.

Our ability to think is at the root of real work and accomplishment. Our ability to choose presupposes a need to think through our alternatives or our choices. It is through our struggles with our thoughts— with that greatest of efforts that we grow. It is through the great wisdom or God, nature or the universe that we are endowed with this most precious of gifts. As we understand and master this gift we hold the key to human growth and improvement.

In *The Quantum Organization* we allow people to choose—we find opportunities for people to choose—we insist that they exercise their free choice at every opportunity and we reap the benefits. It is in our nature to grow through choice. Does it not stand to reason that top-down, command-and-control organizational structures that take away much of our choices are unnatural? Does it not also stand to reason that processes that push us into dull corners of rote actions and memorized activities are enemies of growth and development? If I can convince you of nothing else in this book beyond the absolute necessity of choice, I will be satisfied.

INTRODUCING MANAGED CHAOS

We know that equilibrium kills creativity. Therefore, there is value in introducing a little chaos into the team to stimulate creative thinking. Robert Kriegel tells us "If It Ain't Broke Break it"[4] and Marcus Buckingham extols us to "First Break All the Rules."[5] Both are metaphors for introducing change into our lives and not allowing old rules, conventional wisdom, and limiting process to govern our lives— at work or elsewhere.

In our control groups we discovered that when we moved people into new jobs just when they were getting comfortable in the work that they were doing, we experienced huge spurts of creativity and we ignited renewed passion for the work. We learned that when people got comfortable in their work they went into an autopilot of sorts—they

4. Robert Kriegel (1991) *If It Ain't Broke Break It*, Warner Books.
5. Marcus Buckingham (1999) *First Break All the Rules*, Simon and Schuster.

shut down their creative engine. They surmised (most often subconsciously) that they had the job "nailed" and there was nothing new to learn, nothing left to fix, and nothing more to improve—things were running smoothly and heaven forbid don't touch anything lest it break.

The simple act of introducing some uncertainty, some managed chaos if you will, into the business lives of our team caused them to develop new stretch goals, question processes, and challenge themselves just to simply learn the business. It was something to watch; books came out and requests for training classes came in—we experienced a flurry of learning almost immediately. The energy was thick and electric.

In short, placing people into uncertain situations causes a natural creative drive to understand the new landscape and to develop fresh ways in which the person can be successful. It may just be the easiest and most cost-efficient way to gain immediate huge productivity benefits—it certainly was for us.

THE KEYS TO GOVERNING COMPLEX SYSTEMS

We know that the key to managing complex systems is to identify and manage strange attractors. We know from earlier discussion that strange attractors are those few basic and foundational components of a complex system that when managed will deliver form and beauty to the system. Simply put, we must find the three or four fundamental driving principles of a system and when we focus attention on them, the rest of the structure will take care of itself. Here are a couple of examples:

Manage Organizations

Set the mission, engage the strategy, change the language, and organize for learning.

Manage a Project

Set the goal, establish the high-level tasks, assign responsibility, and establish accountability.

In both of these cases all that is necessary for the manager to deliver the desired outcomes is to manage the strange attractors rigorously. As in "Manage a Project" above, we often feel we need to manage every little task in the project. Our project tools such as Microsoft's Project 2000 scream for us to manage the minutia. I think Project 2000 is a fine tool and I use it a lot. But just because you can track it does not mean that it must be tracked. Just because it can be measured does not mean that it must be measured. In fact, if you manage at too low a level, with too much detail, you exponentially increase the complexity of the project manager's job. Remember: nurture and care for the roots of the tree, and the leaves will develop with form and beauty.

Use the following three techniques to help determine the strange attractors of a complex system. Remember that this effort is as much an art as a science.

1. Use pictures and drawings to chart out the complex system to at least three to four levels of depth. I like to use flow diagrams: they help me see the relationships of one task to another. Study the diagrams until you see the natural roots of the system. These are your strange attractors.
2. Once you have identified these foundations of your system, study them in depth—learn everything that you can about these threads that run the length of your project or task. Build new flow diagrams and drawings of these critical components to insure that you have uncovered everything there is to know about them.
3. Manage what you have discovered as if your professional life depends upon it—perhaps it does. At the core of this management is communication. Make it perfectly clear to everyone remotely involved exactly what you are managing, what your expectations are, who is accountable, and what your timeline is—then let the project unfold in all its glory.

The first or second time you attempt this, it may create great uncertainty within you. Have faith and wait for the outcome. Some of the rewards to you will be:

- Better project quality.
- More time returned to you for other things.
- More meaningful work for your teams.
- Increased growth in your people.
- A flood of creative thought from individuals and groups.

When you have built your skills and capabilities at uncovering and defining your strange attractors you will have achieved one of the great benefits of *The Quantum Organization*. When you see how simple this is and how the complexity of systems melts before your eyes you will ask yourself how it is that you did not see this before.

THE DIFFERENCES BETWEEN DIALOG AND DEBATE

Dialog, or the exploration of ideas through dialog, is foundational to our new organization and management practice as we create an exchange of ideas with the purpose of creating a third (improved) solution. Let's quickly review the rules for dialog that we introduced in chapter 8.

1. Spend time teaching your teams what dialog is (and is not).
2. Post the rules for engaging in dialog in your meeting rooms and offices.
3. Aggressively follow the rules for dialog.
4. As a leader/manager remember that your voice is simply one of many with equal weight—act accordingly.
5. Allow others to facilitate meetings—use pop-up leadership (see chapter 3—self-forming teams).
6. Use the techniques described in chapter 3 to stimulate creativity.
7. Draw out the quiet people.
8. Follow a discussion thread until discussion around this thread has been exhausted, regardless of the tangents you may go down (see rule 4).
9. Do not watch the clock. If you have to extend the meeting time or reconvene another meeting then do so. Remember, the objective is to tap into the knowledge and wisdom of the group, not meet time-lines.
10. Encourage each other (see rule 1).

The most effective role you as a manager must play is that of dialog facilitator. It takes but a short amount of time for your teams to catch the spirit of dialog (vs debate) if you set the correct tone and the right example. As a facilitator you can do these five things to insure successful dialog:

1. Take time at the beginning of each meeting to review the rules of the meeting. Be diligent in stopping the meeting to reinforce the rules of dialog.

2. *Do not* engage in debate yourself—set the proper example. Avoid the pitfall of assuming that because you are the management leader that you know more than anyone in the room. Spend more of your time with your mouth closed and your ears open.
3. Work with key people outside of meetings to get their buy in and their assistance in supporting you as facilitator (let's call them dialog champions). Having a few champions not only supporting dialog by their example, but also helping to counter (educate) peers that are not following the rules of dialog helps tremendously.
4. Keep in mind that the objective of the meeting is ALWAYS to take the information and options that are currently on the table to form a new and improved solution. This may not always happen but it is always the goal. Insure that this object is clear and re-iterated.
5. When you feel that you have a team that is effective at dialog, invite others as observers to learn from the team. This is quite good and inexpensive training.

If people, *your* people, find themselves in an environment where their undeveloped thoughts are received with anticipation instead of antagonism and ridicule you will find the flow of ideas and solutions almost too much to keep straight. We found that time and time again we had too many new ideas and solutions to address—a side effect of dialog that quite frankly I am willing to live with. We did, however, recognize the frustration that employees have when their good ideas go unrealized for long periods of time. We addressed this problem by doing the following:

1. We established a database of ideas that we published online.
2. We included the person's name and department along with the substance of the idea. This instilled a small sense of being "published" and gave the contributor a feeling of self-satisfaction.
3. We gave the contributor some very quick and frank feedback regarding their idea, such as: great idea we are moving forward with it; does not fit with strategic goals; budget will not allow for it this year, etc. This avoided the problem of the submitter thinking that his idea went into a black hole never to be seen again.
4. We adopted a policy of rewarding good ideas as they progressed through the system with large rewards for ideas that were implemented and delivered results.

All in all while it is impossible to take on every idea that employees submit, with good, crisp, and timely communications most employees were satisfied with the process and continued to contribute new and fresh ideas.

Chapter 11

Creativity is King (or Queen)

I am enough of an artist to draw freely upon my imagination. Imagination is more important than knowledge. Knowledge is limited. Imagination encircles the world. [1]

TAP INTO THE CREATIVE SUBCONSCIOUS

In chapter 2 we learned that scientists believe that:

1. The subconscious thinks in pictures and images.
2. The subconscious never sleeps.
3. The subconscious mind records everything it sees or hears.
4. The subconscious can be given tasks.

The list you have just read contains some of the most important pieces of information that you will need on your way to crafting a more creative organization—a more creative you. Items 1, 2, and 3 are exceptionally fascinating characteristics of the human subconscious mind, but number 4, the fact that the subconscious can be given tasks, is the real pearl in the list. Items 1, 2, and 3 are ideas that you may just have to accept as facts. It may take research and technical capabilities beyond your ability or desire to undertake in order to prove 1, 2, and 3 to be true. But, you can verify number 4 with relative ease each and every day as you put it to the test.

Also in chapter 2 we learned how to tap into the other-than-conscious mind. Let's review that list of seven steps briefly here:

1. Create one-page documents that through pictures, images, and descriptive text pose questions—problems to be solved.
2. Review these descriptive queries on a regular basis—at least once daily.

3. Set aside time to ponder and allow the subconscious to work on the problem(s).
4. Sleep on it.
5. Be receptive to those flashes of learning, the sudden intuitive perception or insight in the essential meaning of something.
6. Record what you have learned, what the subconscious is telling you, and begin working on your action plans.
7. Use this process over and over again—this is as much or more an art as it is a science.

My personal experience and the outcomes of our trial groups that put this concept to the test demonstrate that the idea of putting a task to the subconscious mind reaps generous rewards. In my personal efforts to build myself into the type of leader and person that I wanted to be, I wrote several of the one-page papers as described in our list above. These "one-pagers" started by establishing a high-level target or goal, defining the objective of the target ("What is it specifically I expect to be or to be able to do?"), next came a clear description of the destination ("What will it look like when I arrive at the target?"). The final element is a clearly articulated description of what I ultimately expect to accomplish (affirmations). Let me demonstrate this with several personal examples of when I followed the seven steps identified above.

Example 1

Target
Become a Great Leader.

Objective of the target
Engage in the evolutionary process that will transform me into a great leader.

What is the destination?
I want to engage in the lifelong adventure of discovery. I want to lead people through that adventure. I want to be the catalyst that will transform people into the best that they can be.

Depict the event
I see a time when I have complete self-awareness. I know my strengths and I know and compensate for my weaknesses. I have the inertia to

over/

transform myself into the leader that is consistent with my principles and values. I have the sense to unlearn erroneous lessons. I have a sense of this business and have an intuitive "dead reckoning" for the course that leads to success. I have a vision for what I want in life, a passion for my work. I conduct myself with integrity in all that I do. I trust people first, last, and always. I have a need to learn and a curiosity and daring in the pursuit of learning. I love to read and often I write about the profound things that I discover. I listen to myself because I know that the still-small voice will not lead me astray.

Example 2

Target
Become an Effective Executive.

Objective of the target
Become very effective and efficient in my journey to contribute to the success of the company.

What is the destination?
I see myself as a very time-efficient and focused executive. I feel good about the work I complete in a day. I significantly affect the results of the organization in a positive way.

Depict the event
I am an effective executive. I attend very few meetings because I have delegated the work to its lowest level. I include in my day personal time for self-development and thought. I am concerned with the results of the organization so I look outside my department for opportunities to help. I have defined organizational values to insure focus on the goals of the company. I make each person's job demanding and big to allow him or her to rise to the challenge. I focus on what people can do and create jobs to maximize their talents. In this spirit, I am willing to put up with weakness in order to get at strength. I hold people accountable for their work. I set priorities.

Example 3

Target
Face Your Fears and Do it Anyway.

Objective of the target
Be able to face my fears head-on without taking extraordinary actions to avoid what must be done.

What is the destination?
I see myself using my fears as a source of power and as self-esteem builders. I am no longer paralyzed by my fears.

Depict the event
I am making phone calls without the dread of making a contact. I am making assignments to people in my callings and work roles without the fear of how they will react. I will introduce myself to new people or old acquaintances without the fear of rejection paralyzing my attempts. I will be able to walk up to my boss and others in authority over me and engage them in simple conversations. I am able to give frank and direct feedback to friends, peers, and subordinates regardless of the positive or negative nature of that feedback.

Example 4

Target
Build an Effective Work Spirit.

Objective of the target
I want to instill a spirit of worthwhile work, ownership, and congratulations in my workgroup and in as many other groups as I can.

What is the destination?
I see a place where work is truly integrated into the soul, into the higher self. This is a place where work is seen as a necessary pillar of self-esteem and self-worth.

over/

Depict the event
In my group I know that my work is worthwhile. I know how my work makes the world a better place. I have defined my values and I know what they are. I never willingly violate them. I am in charge of achieving my goals. I know what my jobs are, I measure my progress, and I take responsibility for achieving success. I have a lot of work, but I am able to complete it. I feel good about the work I do at the end of the day. I congratulate others. There is a great rewards system in place and I feel that my efforts are appreciated. I applaud my progress as well as my achievements.

Example 5

Target
Build an Organization Upon Innovation.

Objective of the target
Insure that I drive innovation across the entire enterprise to create value.

What is the destination?
I see a time when I am recognized as the best innovative thinker in the company. I am building cross-enterprise personal networks, engaged in accelerated learning, and I am delivering state-of-the-art expertise.

Depict the event
I see myself building competency platforms in the organization around technology, knowledge and learning, leadership, innovation and development, and performance growth. I am conducting analyses to identify gaps in the business. I am building a roadmap of emerging technologies and mapping them to business opportunities. I have built robust scenarios and supporting contingency plans. I have developed and promoted a compelling business vision and it is tied to strategy. I have successfully developed a partnership mentality in the company and we are adding value through those partnerships. Everyone has a clear purpose and knows their role. I have championed Performance Improvement Teams to maximize efficiency.

The outcomes for each of these five examples was amazing and personally stunning. In all examples I followed the seven steps with diligence and with careful attention to detail. While I may not be the final and most objective judge as to how well I have achieved all the targets that I set for myself, I will say that I am totally pleased with all the results. Let me share some of my learning and experiences with this most powerful of tools:

- In my quest to become a better leader I have developed an ongoing trust for my instincts and that includes evaluating people. As a result of daily contemplation and meditation I have continued to examine my values and deepened my resolve to be true to those values and to integrate them almost subconsciously into my daily work activities. This renewed confidence is a byproduct of knowing that my subconscious mind will accept tasks and deliver solutions even when things are unclear and no resolution is obvious.
- I continue to have a thirst for knowledge and new learning. I regularly develop flashes of insight regarding how to apply the new things that I have learned to the business and personal issues of the day. My ability to recall and apply the concepts and techniques that I learn continues to amaze.
- I have virtually eliminated all of my preconditioning with regard to my fears related to new and uncertain situations. Not only am I unafraid of meeting new people, I have also developed a desire to meet others regardless of their station in life. I have integrated "meeting new people and understanding who they are" as part of my lifelong learning plan.
- I am finally at peace with the interrelated nature of my work life and my personal life—there is only life. I am constantly delivered from my subconscious mind new and fresh ideas that are a product of the data and information that I feed my mind and the specific act of challenging my other-than-conscious mind to apply that knowledge to the everyday problems at hand.
- I have become the person that I wanted to become. I do not claim to have arrived at some notion of personal perfection, but I have achieved the goals and targets that I set for myself—I have many more goals yet ahead of me. I have engaged my subconscious mind and I see the benefits daily.

You will of course want to prove these concepts to yourself—I challenge you to do it. The benefits of harnessing the power of the subconscious mind will materially change your life—it has mine.

POWER THROUGH PICTURES AND IMAGES

From chapter 2 we know that the subconscious mind works in pictures and images. Picture and images are the most effective way to communicate with the other-than-conscious mind. We also know that the subconscious mind's workings are analogous to a computer. Requests and tasks are fed into the computer in a format that the machine understands. The tasks are processed until a solution is reached. This knowledge of the inner workings of the subconscious mind is a source of personal power to you. Understanding the great untapped resources of the mind and putting them to work for you is a priceless endowment, one that must be put to use every minute of your life.

To take advantage of our other-than-conscious mind we must communicate with powerful visual and descriptive images, pictures, color, and graphics—they communicate so much and create a lasting image in the mind long after the text has faded. There are several ways in which we can introduce more visuals and graphic descriptions into our work:

- Communicate with tools such as Microsoft PowerPoint instead of word processors. Use fewer words—more bullet points; use more pictures—charts and graphs; associate appropriate clipart with each bullet point.
- Use posters and banners to communicate mission and vision statements or your top-ten priorities. Use very few words and no sentences. Find powerful pictures or images (or create your own) that elicit a strong emotional response related to your vision.
- Adopt an icon or other visual that represents your culture or strategy and use it on every written communication, e-mail, memo, or report.
- In chapter 3 we discussed using physical models as creative tools to generate ideas. Use models to communicate ideas as well. Build models to help convey the essence of your business plans, individual business cases, and strategies.

One of the most powerful creative experiences I ever had was while using models to convey a message. In 1999 and 2000 our strategy team (one of the control groups used in gathering the research for this book) determined that investing in a new start-up venture made sense for the company. After months of research and analysis a plan was developed and was about ready to present to executive management for approval. The team felt particularly militant about how important this new venture was to the healthy future of the company and wanted to be sure that we were able to convey that sense to the executive team.

After much dialog on the subject of how best to communicate our passion around this new business opportunity we decided to build a model to help us impart the most important points of our plan. During our dialog session we decided to use an ocean-going oil-drilling platform as a metaphor for our business plan. The oilrig was symbolic of our venture in several ways:

- The oil derrick was a beacon or an anchor point in uncertain waters.
- There were many potential pitfalls that were lurking beneath the waters, not entirely visible from the surface.
- There was great wealth and opportunity associated with great risk.
- Sometimes the ocean was calm and certain and at other times great winds and waves crashed against the structure. The rig and its crew needed to be prepared to weather these storms and uncertainties.
- It took many people working in concert with precision to operate the rig and help it to reach its goal.

We decided that, as this project was so important, we would contract out the building of the final model to a professional firm (these are the people that build the scale models of towns and buildings for architectural firms). In order to transfer our thinking and expectations to the modelers we worked with an artist to help us draw out and design the essence of our thinking. In short, it worked out great. The model had progressive lighting that we could control remotely to highlight the various portions of the model allowing us to describe each aspect of the model and therefore our business plan. The model did its job. It was certainly eye catching and seized the attention of all who saw it. It swiftly helped convey through graphic image and metaphor the essence of our plan and the risks and rewards. A verbal or textual message that was as content rich and potent would have taken an enormous amount of time and required reams of paper—and would not have been near as effective.

Pictures and images are a most effective way to connect with the other-than-conscious mind—yours or the minds of others. They send powerful yet at times simple messages that are rich with content and more easily understood, especially within diverse groups of people. Controlling the vast resources of the mind and putting them to work for you can be put into practice every day of your life.

CONSTRUCTING A NEW LANGUAGE

Pictures and images are powerful tools but this is not to say that words do not play an important creative role as well. Words and language are absolutely critical in the transformation process towards *The Quantum Organization*. Constructing a new language does not imply that we invent new words, dialects, or an entire new tongue. But you must create, from the words that you know, new phrases that can be linked to the images and ideas that you create—that can be linked to your new leadership paradigm. A key to integrating your message, or your mission, throughout your organization is the creation this new language, new words that evoke an emotional response and specific visual images tied to goals and your aspirations for your teams.

In other words, carefully select the words that are important to you and assign to them new meaning—meaning that will help you communicate your message. Here are some examples:

Example 1

Old Organization
Leadership: Top-down, command-and-control methodology. Perquisites and benefits ascribed to a few. Those at the top are brighter and more capable than those that are further down in the organization.

Quantum Organization
Leadership: Pop-up leadership. Many people with many skills brought together to solve problems. Leaders recognize that the individual is key to the success of the organization.

Example 2

Old Organization
Productivity: Tightly controlled process that is predictable; where deviation from the process is bad. Making all people conform to this "best practice" regardless of the individual's skills or abilities. Hiring people that fit the process.

Quantum Organization
Productivity: Evolving the process to fit the talents of the people. Hiring "athletes" vs "position players." Management encourages people to work creatively outside the process to improve and evolve the process.

Example 3

Old Organization
Learning: In the old organization learning equates to training. This means training people in the existing process—throwing in some technical training for good measure.

Quantum Organization
Learning: Learning is a lifelong endeavor. Management values well-rounded individuals and encourages learning at all levels and in many disciplines. The management also recognizes the link between positive self-image (self-esteem) and the pursuit of knowledge.

These are just three examples of the dozens of words and expressions to which you must assign new definitions. As you and your teams use these words and phrases in new ways it will invoke those most important images of your new leadership and organizational paradigm—*The Quantum Organization.*

In *The Quantum Organization* capturing the power of the subconscious mind is key to our new leadership model—the wellspring of our potential. This is where we get those inventive, creative new ideas that will drive real value for the company and for people. Again let me say, people are a company's greatest asset, its most valued resource. It is up to us to prove it, to demonstrate the value of the individual through superior creativity leading to extraordinary output.

Chapter 12

The Formula for Success: S=EPOC; Success=Energy*Passion*Ownership* Creativity

If one advances confidently in the direction of his dreams and endeavors to live the life which he has imagined, he will meet with a success unexpected in common hours.[1]

INTRODUCTION

As a young boy, I used to love to watch the Popeye cartoon. Popeye was the good guy. He was strong and fit and he was afraid of nothing—just how I imagined a guy should be. Of course I learned since then that it is OK to show that more sensitive side. I am not sure Popeye would have totally approved, but times change and people change, and it is tough work getting in touch with your sensitive side— I am not so sure my childhood hero could make it in this world of apparent contradictions.

What intrigued me about Popeye was his can of spinach. I never tasted the stuff until I was twenty years old (thank goodness, I am not sure I could survive another childhood emotional scar), but it did not matter what it tasted like—Popeye liked it and it made him strong. Being strong was good: it saved the day, it saved the girl, and it came with big muscles.

Since the days of my youth opening that can of spinach became a metaphor for reaching deep down into your gut and finding that intestinal fortitude, that extra effort, that last ounce of energy needed to go over the top—to deliver the results. In this chapter I want to introduce

1. Henry David Thorea, www.housequotes.com

a formula for great success—the recipe that is in our can of spinach so to speak. It depends upon four components that when multiplied by each other can deliver the most amazing results. E*P*O*C (energy, passion, ownership, creativity) is a potent way to approach problem solving and creative thinking. Approaching challenges at work and home with passion and creativity brings about unique solutions and a zest for work, for family, and for life.

ENERGY, PASSION, OWNERSHIP, AND CREATIVITY

Let's start with some simple definitions for E*P*O*C.

- *Energy*: the equivalent of the adrenaline burst that leads to heroic deeds. It has physical, intellectual, and emotional aspects.
- *Passion*: the highest level of involvement, which dominates your awareness, thoughts, desires. We feel passionate about people, things, and ideas that matter the most to us. Passion can bring out the best in us.
- *Ownership*: this is about seeing things through. It is about coming to the realization that nobody is coming to solve your problems or to make you happy—you must do it yourself. Recognizing that you are responsible for how you react and respond to others, for how you feel, for what you want, and for what you think.
- *Creativity*: thinking out of the box. It is the ability to see relationships and connections that others don't see and which you didn't previously see. Todd Siler says this is about "seeing through things."[2]

Bringing a markedly increased focus (opening our can—E*P*O*C) to a problem requires much physical energy and emotional effort. This level of effort is not sustainable over a long period of time. In fact, it is not even appropriate or wise to carry on this increased effort beyond the moment. Just as Popeye only opened his can, his reserves if you will, during those moments when it was most needed, we too must selectively decide when it is appropriate to bring an increased level of energy, emotion, leadership, and aggression to our problems and tasks—to open our can figuratively.

In chapter 7 we were introduced to a description of a picture of a woman dressed in business attire with a sledgehammer in her hands. If you recall, she was taking aim at the glass ceiling above her head. Walking on top of the ceiling and in clear view from her vantage point

2. Todd Siler (1997) *Think Like a Genius*, Bantam Books.

were the stereotypical male executives dressed in gray suits and totally oblivious to what was happening down below. The expression on
the woman's face was focused—filled with confident determination—
she had opened her can.

I think those who signed the American Declaration of Independence
surely took up their task with energy, passion, ownership, and creativity—they opened their can.

We have the example from the bible when Jesus Christ drove the
moneychangers from the temple[3]—he certainly had opened his can.

There is a great story of a General of the Army in ancient times—
he surely picked a great moment to open his can. This general was the
chief commander of all the armies of his people. While he and his sol-
diers were away fighting for the freedom of the people he learned of a
great rebellion back home. Some selfish men had taken advantage of
the weakened state of affairs and had overthrown the government
back home. When the general heard of this traitorous act he took his
cloak and he wrote upon it—"In memory of our God, our religion, and
freedom, and our peace, our wives, and our children"—and he fastened
it upon the end of a pole. Then he put on his head-plate and his armor.
He took up his shield, took the pole and the cloak (he called it the title
of liberty) and went among his people, waving this title of liberty in
the air so all could see the writing, saying: "Whomever will maintain
this title of freedom upon this land, let them come now and make a
pledge that they will maintain their rights, and their religion, and their
freedoms from those that would destroy them." And when he did this
the people came running together with their armor and their shields
pledging their allegiance to this cause.

History is replete with many more examples of courageous men and
women who, when the chips were down, reached deep down inside for
that extra effort that made a difference. We see this going on all
around us—men and women rising to the occasion to get work done.
Often times these pivotal moments just happen without much thought
or planning; the timing is right and someone opens their can in order
to move the group to the next level. But, this is too powerful a tool to
be left to chance.

It is time to explore how and when we open our can.

WHEN DO YOU OPEN YOUR CAN?

You open your can when you are seeking innovative/creative ways to
solve business and/or personal challenges. Since your can gets at least

3. *The Bible*, King James Version, Mark 11:15–17.

partially emptied every time you open it, and it takes time to refill it, you can't leave it open all the time or too often. You open your can when working harder or simply doing more is not enough and you need to work or do differently. Here is a checklist to help you know when you should open your can as opposed to just working harder.

- The light at the end of the tunnel turns out to be a train coming at you.
- Your emotional state seems out of proportion to what is objectively happening.
- Risk associated with not being successful is very large (e.g. bankruptcy, permanently damaged relationships, big projects).
- You recognize that you're in one of those situations when, as Einstein put it so deftly, "Problems cannot be solved at the same level of awareness that created them."[4]
- When you're repeatedly playing the victim.
- When you're stuck.
- When your usual way of managing things, dealing with problems, etc. is no longer working or being successful.
- When you're under severe stress—physical, emotional, job, etc.
- When you need to "cut in your afterburner" to get up to speed really quickly.
- When you need to inspire others to attain that which they thought was unattainable.

WHAT IS IN YOUR CAN?

Your can is like a toolbox. The type of tool that is used is dependent upon the situation (personal or business). In addition to E*P*O*C everyone's toolbox contains additional elements such as:

- Business planning templates (marketing finance, strategy, operations).
- Sources of strength/support (faith, family, friends).
- Network of professional resources.
- Qualitative and quantitative intelligence (data, analysis).
- Skills/competencies.
- Innovative ideas.
- Your spiritual self.
- Your best.

4. Albert Einstein, www.houseofquotes.com

WHY DO YOU NEED A CAN?

There will be situations in which you have tried doing the usual things to drive a group over the top and it does not work. Remember Popeye and his spinach—sometimes the situation calls for new techniques or even drastic measures.

It is important to realize that there are rules, structures, components, techniques, tools, and risks that apply to opening your can. Also, the ability to open your can is not something that some people have and some do not; rather, it is something that can be learned. And once learned, you can carry it with you wherever you go.

HOW DO YOU FILL YOUR CAN?

You fill your can by continuously seeking opportunities to learn and to replenish your spirit or your soul. This allows us to fill our cans with new tools, both personal and professional.

- *Take the time to nourish and replenish yourself*—feed your mind—expand your interests—read.
- *Reflection*—re-examine yourself, your goals, and revisit your passions.
- *Relaxation*—do something that truly feeds your soul. This could be a hobby or something that gets you in touch with some of your personal passions.
- *Exercise/nutrition*—caring for your body helps replenish your energy level.
- *Connect with friends*—the support of others can help build ownership, because, although no one is coming to solve your problems, no one has to go it alone. Ownership is not "alone ship."

HOW DO YOU OPEN YOUR CAN?

Once you recognize that you need to open your can, it can be helpful to get to a new place physically, emotionally, and intellectually before you open it. Get up and change where you are physically located to underscore the need to change what you're doing. A trip to the water cooler, walking around the block, sitting in a different chair facing a different direction—all can help put you in the mindset to open your can.

If your emotions are governing—either positive or negative—rein them in. Deep breathing, meditating if you have time, talking to someone who can truly listen to help you get clear. Opening your can is an intellectual, problem-solving exercise. But hang on to what's underlying that emotion so that you can use it as an energy source; redirect the energy you are expending on the emotion onto solving the problem.

If you're stuck in a non-productive mindset, get out of it. Focus on opportunities and possibilities, not obstacles and impossibilities. Keep the focus on "What can I do," not "What I cannot do." Be an owner, not a victim.

IF YOU DO NOT OPEN YOUR CAN, WHO WILL?

Opening your can must be a self-directed exercise, a call to action. Because the content of everyone's can is different, only you can decide when and where to open your can. While no one can open it for us, and no one can make us open it, sometimes we need help opening our can. Part of opening your can may involve asking for help or advice. Remember: do not ask for advice if you are not willing to consider it seriously (and do not offer advice if you cannot accept that it might not be used).

HOW TO USE WHAT IS IN YOUR CAN

Opening your can must be a conscious, reasoned response to the situation or need; you cannot just open your can any and every time something goes wrong or presents a challenge. You must not overreact.

Often it will help to talk to someone, or a small group to get another view(s) on whether opening your can is what is really needed in a situation. Can someone else help? Are you just overlooking something that is obvious to someone else?

Be clear on the problem or situation to make sure that you unleash E*P*O*C in the right direction.

You must first clarify:

- What is the objective of the situation?
- What do I think, feel, or want in a response?
- What are the consequences of not opening the can?

WHERE DO YOU OPEN YOUR CAN?

Eventually you have to bring your open can to the problem, wherever it is. However, the actual opening of your can and tapping into E*P*O*C can happen in different places. You can look at this question in terms of whether you're alone or in a group, or whether you are at work or in a personal situation:

- *In private*: there can be times when you need to be alone to open your can. Sometimes it is a matter of personal reflection—building the resolve to do what has to be done.
- *In public*: if the situation requires immediate response, break out your can! But remember, you need to come from a calm, well-thought-out place. If you cannot get there, you may need to call a time out.
- *At home/in your personal life*: because of the emotions we invest in our family and friends, this can be a very hard place to open your can and do something radically different. However, the rewards can be great. Perseverance will be necessary because these situations are most likely to be about relationships, and the other person(s) in the relationship will normally resist change.
- *At work*: imagine working at a place where you could tap into the same energy and enthusiasm you feel about your family, hobby, or other personal passions to solve problems. Imagine being able to bring the creativity with which you greet life to problem solving at work. Opening your can at work can revolutionize not only your work experience but also your life.

HOW DO YOU FIND YOUR CAN?

Finding your personal can (I have been accused of not being able to hit my can with either hand) is as much about courage and determination as anything else. You must look deep inside yourself, take that long look in the mirror and decide here and now that you will work with energy, that you will find the passion that drives you, that you will take ownership for getting things done, and that you will think with a renewed creativity—think outside the box as the saying goes.

CAUTION: WARNING LABEL ON YOUR CAN

When you open your can, you will be doing things differently than usual. People will not know how to respond to you, they may be confused, resistant, and even hostile. Know that these reactions may happen, be prepared for them. It may help to let people know in advance what you are doing so that they have a chance to understand; doing so may reduce their adverse reactions, but it may not eliminate them.

When you open your can, even you will not know what the outcome will be. Be prepared for the unexpected and the unknown. This situation can create uncertainty, but the results will be astonishing. Like a roller coaster, opening your can is both frightening and fun. When you're finished, you will want to ride it again.

I hope you have had as much fun with the image of Popeye and his can of spinach as I have. I like it because it is a very clear metaphor for the concepts and principles of applying energy, passion, ownership, and creativity to your work and to your life.

Section II Summary

- There is no greater asset one can bring to a problem than the unencumbered mind.

- Using pictures we were able to evoke a tremendous emotional connection between a person and a concept.

- There are several books that are a must read on the way to reaching a more complete understanding of how the models of the universe can help us manage and run our lives.

- Dr. Nathaniel Branden describes self-esteem as "confidence in our ability to think, confidence in our ability to cope with the basic challenges of life."

- To unleash a creative fountainhead requires confidence, poise, self-assurance, and many similar characteristics—in other words, a positive self-image.

- The key to a positive self-image is triggered by real work and real accomplishment.

- Critical to staying in harmony with the team and with nature is a pure delight in the accomplishment of others.

- There are six ways you can drive increased productivity by building individual self-esteem through work:

  1. Always have meaningful goals. Insure that the goals are measurable, achievable, and have a stretch element.
  2. Insure that all work is clearly linked to strategic and operational plans. Each person should know exactly how the work that he or she is engaged in helps the company achieve its goals.
  3. Reward achievement of goals in ways that are meaningful to the individual. Some would consider a lunch or dinner with the Chairman a great treat. Others would count this event as the ultimate torture.

4. Do not allow the poor performance of some workers to destroy the morale and esteem of others. In other words, handle your performance problems swiftly and fairly.
5. Be careful with perks and benefits that further widen the gap between management and staff. By this I mean err on the side of conservatism by limiting if not eliminating huge lavish offices, separate facilities (i.e. dining, lavatory, health) for management and staff, reserved parking, materially better health benefits, and so on.
6. Take joy in the success of others. Give credit where credit is due and for heaven's sake do not take credit for other people's work!

■ Recognizing the deeds of others and building excitement within the team for individual and team success delivers huge paybacks. We implemented a five-step program for recognizing and supporting each other:

1. Provide a shadow leader for each person. Sometimes in the legal profession this is called second chair (I know this from watching episodes of *The Practice*–this officially makes me dangerous). The shadow leader provides encouragement, advice and council, and that much-needed emotional support.
2. Understand what kind of recognition that the individual desires or responds to. Some respond to monetary rewards and others to personal congratulations while still others enjoy added responsibilities. Remember, what motivates you does not necessarily motivate the next person.
3. Make sure that every person in the organization knows what the team strategy and goals are and link every piece of work an individual is responsible for to those goals and strategies.
4. Align compensation plans around team goals. The teams must be natural teams with a lot in common. Making everyone part of one great big team is not effective; in fact it is detrimental and drives selfishness and nonconformist behavior.
5. Implement a program to define the key processes in the organization (strange attractors) and to execute on those processes with precision and excellence. This gave us something to cheer about.

■ There are two techniques that are quite simple yet almost miraculous in their value and benefit to a learning program:

1. Asking Questions.
2. Writing Answers.

CHAPTER 8

■ A *Quantum Organization* is a learning organization.

■ Your challenge is to introduce people to the fun and excitement of learning new things—to expanding their field of view.

■ My experience led me to develop my top priorities—the Vital Five:

1. There was very little learning going on with this group. Everyone was stale. There was no reason let alone an opportunity to learn and grow.
2. Management's expectations of employees did not match customer expectations of the company.
3. There was no ownership being taken by management or employees for the success of the business.
4. The lack of leadership towards a clear vision had sapped the energy of the people.
5. In general, the management lacked the business management skills necessary to run this business effectively (or any business for that matter).

■ Too much term in job breeds complacency, a lack of creativity, boredom, and the misguided thinking that there is nothing left to learn.

■ Introducing some calculated and managed chaos into the business is a key stratagem for a learning organization.

■ The most effective tactic for building a learning organization is building expectations of learning.

■ Leading IS by example.

■ Set aside time to read, both on the job and off the job.

■ Spending time together and reasoning out solutions to problems, engaging in the creative process, and simply engaging in free-form discussion is a cornerstone characteristic of *The Quantum Organization*.

■ The nature of dialog is unstructured. It is from this unstructured quality that we are able to tap into the hidden knowledge that exists within us all.

- The still-small voice is a real source of knowledge, insight, and power.

CHAPTER 9

- Some characteristics of *The Quantum Organization* are better accomplished through evolution.

- Planting seeds is one technique that is invaluable in beginning the evolution to a more quantum-like model.

- Meeting strategies:

    - As the organizational leader of the team I wanted to resist the urge to take control of the meeting and establish myself as the focal point of discussion. I would allow and encourage pop-up leaders to emerge.
    - I would use silence (my silence) as a tool to encourage participation.
    - I would have no agenda.
    - I would assume the responsibility of ensuring a balanced participation between all participants.
    - I would enforce the no-debate—only dialog rule.

- *The Quantum Organization* is about getting in touch with our true nature and organizing and executing our work in harmony with that nature.

CHAPTER 10

- Some characteristics of *The Quantum Organization* are better accomplished through revolution.

- It is time to dramatically change some of our most sacred fundamentals that have been cornerstones to our management philosophy of the past 100-plus years:

    - Top-down, command-and-control management and complex hierarchical organization structures are inefficient and are roadblocks to human creativity—they must go and go now.
    - Not only is the command-and-control management practice

inefficient, it absolutely stifles human growth—men and women grow and increase only through their own agency.

- Machine-like, assembly-line operations are the kiss of death to growth and learning—the introduction of a little managed chaos into an organization is absolutely necessary.
- Managing complex systems starts from the bottom up and not from the top down—strange attractors are the key to managing complex systems.
- Debate and other competitive techniques for drawing out and exploring new ideas clearly stand in the way of personal expression and idea generation—it is time for dialog to replace debate.

- Self-forming teams need these five things in order to take root and grow:

  1. A clearly developed problem statement or goal.
  2. Well-communicated and understood ground rules for the teams.
  3. Team members with the ability to thrive in unstructured organizational environments.
  4. Patient and supportive management.
  5. Measurements of success.

- The ground rules for self-forming teams are:

  - Anyone can lead the team.
  - There is no voting for team leadership.
  - A leader will emerge through the normal course of dialog and discussion of the problem statement.
  - Be patient—let nature take its course.
  - Take courage—when it feels right for someone to take charge then have the courage to step-up and lead the team.

- Allowing teams to form appropriately may take only a few minutes of the first team meeting; it also may take more than one discussion session.
- Free agency is as much about the process of choosing as it is about the fact that we get to choose.

- We know that equilibrium kills creativity. Therefore, there is value in introducing a little chaos into the team to stimulate creative thinking.

- There are three techniques to help determine the strange attractors of a complex system:

  1. Use pictures and drawings to chart out the complex system to at least three to four levels of depth.
  2. Once you have identified these foundations of your system, study them in depth—learn everything that you can about these threads that run the length of your project or task.
  3. Manage what you have discovered as if your professional life depends upon it—perhaps it does.

- Five things to insure successful dialog:

  1. Take time at the beginning of each meeting to review the rules of the meeting. Be diligent in stopping the meeting to reinforce the rules of dialog.
  2. DO NOT engage in debate yourself—set the proper example. Avoid the pitfall of assuming that because you are the management leader you know more than anyone in the room. Spend more of your time with your mouth closed and your ears open.
  3. Work with key people outside of meetings to get their buy in and their assistance in supporting you as facilitator (let's call them dialog champions). Having a few champions not only supporting dialog by their example, but also helping to counter (educate) peers that are not following the rules of dialog helps tremendously.
  4. Keep in mind that the objective of the meeting is ALWAYS to take the information and options that are currently on the table to form a new and improved solution. This may not always happen but it is always the goal. Insure that this object is overtly clear, obvious, and stated over and over again.
  5. When you feel that you have a team that is effective at dialog, invite others as observers to learn from the team. Quite good and inexpensive training.

CHAPTER 11

- The idea of putting a task to the subconscious mind reaps generous rewards.

- The subconscious mind works in pictures and images.

- The knowledge of the inner workings of the subconscious mind is a source of personal power.
- To take advantage of our other-than-conscious mind we must communicate with powerful visual and descriptive images, pictures, color, and graphics.

- There are several ways in which we can introduce more visuals and graphic descriptions into our work:

    - Communicate with tools such as Microsoft PowerPoint instead of word processors. Use fewer words—more bullet points; use more pictures—charts and graphs; associate appropriate clipart with each bullet point.
    - Use posters and banners to communicate mission and vision statements or your top-ten priorities. Use very few words and NO sentences. Find powerful pictures or images (or create your own) that elicit a strong emotional response related to your vision.
    - Adopt an icon or other visual that represents your culture or strategy and use it on every written communication, e-mail, memo, or report.
    - Use models to communicate ideas. Build models to help convey the essence of your business plans, individual business cases, and strategies.

- Words and language are absolutely critical in the transformation process towards *The Quantum Organization*.

- Constructing a new language does not imply that we invent new words, dialects, or an entire new tongue.

- Create, from the words that you know, new phrases that can be linked to the images and ideas that you create.

CHAPTER 12

- E*P*O*C (energy, passion, ownership, creativity) is a potent way to approach problem solving and creative thinking.

- Definition of E*P*O*C.

    - *Energy*: the equivalent of the adrenaline burst that leads to heroic deeds. It has physical, intellectual, and emotional aspects.

- *Passion*: the highest level of involvement, which dominates your awareness, thoughts, desires. We feel passionate about people, things, and ideas that matter the most to us. Passion can bring out the best in us.
- *Ownership*: ownership is about seeing things through. It is about coming to the realization that nobody is coming to solve your problems or to make you happy—you must do it yourself. Recognizing that you are responsible for how you react and respond to others, for how you feel, for what you want, and for what you think
- *Creativity*: thinking out of the box. It is the ability to see relationships and connections that others do not see and which you didn't previously see. Todd Siler says this is about "seeing through things."[1]

- You open your can when you are seeking innovative/creative ways of solving business and/or personal challenges.

- Your can is like a toolbox. The type of tool that is used is dependent upon the situation (personal or business).

- There are rules, structures, components, techniques, tools, and risks that apply to opening your can.

- You fill your can by continuously seeking opportunities to learn and to replenish your spirit or your soul.

- It can be helpful to get to a new place physically, emotionally, and intellectually before you open your can.

- Opening your can must be a self-directed exercise, a call to action.

- Opening your can must be a conscious, reasoned response to the situation or need.

- You must bring your open can to the problem, wherever it is.

- Finding your personal can is as much about courage and determination as anything else—you must look deep inside yourself.

1. Todd Siler (1997)*Think Like a Genius*, Bantam Books.

Epilogue

IT is not the critic who counts, not the man who points out how the strong man stumbles or where the doer of deeds could have done them better. The credit belongs to the man who is actually in the arena, whose face is marred by dust and sweat and blood, who strives valiantly, who errs and comes short again and again because there is not effort without error and short-comings, who knows the great devotion, who spends himself in a worthy cause, who at best knows in the end the high achievement of triumph and who at worst, if he fails while daring greatly, knows his place shall never be with those timid and cold souls who know neither victory nor defeat.[1]

We have barely scratched the surface of this new leadership model we call *The Quantum Organization*. Nevertheless, it is my hope that we have stirred your thinking just a bit, just enough to start you on a path of exploration and learning.

We have touched on the science that underpins our theories:

1. Quantum physics.
2. Nature of the subconscious mind.
3. Influence of language.
4. Harmony with nature.

We have outlined some tools you can use in your day-to-day work:

1. Dialog.
2. Organizational models.
3. Self-forming teams.
4. Information hubs.

1. Theodore Roosevelt.

5. Metaphorming.
6. Quantum language.
7. Disequilibrium.
8. Strange attractors.

We have talked about the practical application of these principles:

1. In meetings.
2. In organizations.
3. In relationships.
4. In planning.
5. In communicating.
6. In our health and well-being.

I have done my best to deliver the best description of this most wondrous concept described as *The Quantum Organization*. Thomas Huxley reminds us, "There is no greater mistake than the hasty conclusion that opinions are worthless because they are badly argued."

I only ask that if your soul has been stirred just a little by what you have read here. Please explore these topics for yourself in depth. There is too much at stake for you and for the world around you to view these concepts as naught.

Thank you for coming along on this adventure with me. And thank you in advance for your efforts to discover more about our quantum nature and to contribute to the learning.

And finally:

A greater poverty than that caused by money is a poverty of unawareness. Men and women go about the world unaware of the goodness, the beauty, and the glories in it...[2]

Good luck in all that you do.

---

2. Thomas Dreier was born in Durand, Wisconsin 5 May 1884. He was a reporter who eventually became an author, lecturer, and philanthropist.

Articles

In late 2002, I met a man by the name of Joseph Schumacher whose leadership impressed me from the start. He had the talent of being able to balance the delicate nature of what I consider three of the major business imperatives:

- Needs of the business.
- Needs of the customers.
- Quality.

Keeping this three-legged business stool standing is no small task—it is a constant give and take. If too much attention is paid to one of the legs or not enough to another the stool is out of balance and will not stand.

Simply put, Joe had a natural feel for his quantum nature. Joe has a way with people and he has a great sense for the business. I found myself always amazed at what he could accomplish regardless of the resources he had at hand. In fact, it seemed that when his resources were the leanest, Joe's accomplishments were his greatest. Joe did indeed have many talents. One of these talents was writing. Joe published some articles on leadership in several trade publications and with his permission I have included some examples of his work here.

Joe Schumacher is the former Fire Chief, PSAP (public safety answering point) Director, and Coordinator of Disaster and Emergency Preparedness for the Arvada (CO) Fire Protection District. He has over twenty years of fire service experience and served on the Jefferson County E9-1-1 Emergency Telephone Authority Board. He is presently Director of E9-1-1 Texas Operations for Intrado Inc. of Longmont, Colorado.

Credibility is the Key to Winning Co-worker Confidence

"We are what we repeatedly do.
Excellence, then, is not an act but a habit." [1]

A 2,000-word article prepared for:

TONI EDWARDS FINLEY
Editor, Public Safety Communications APCO Bulletin

by:
JOE SCHUMACHER
Intrado Inc., Boulder, Colorado

ABSTRACT

Promotion to supervisor is indeed an endorsement of your core competency as a communicator, organizer, mentor, mediator, and performance evaluator. The key to long-term leadership success, however, lies within your professional credibility. This article provides advice on establishing and maintaining a credibility power base.

SPEAK HONESTLY AND FROM THE HEART

Believability is the beginning and end point when establishing a durable foundation of credibility. So after promotion to Communications Center Supervisor, continue to be yourself without radically changing how you conduct business or interact with co-workers. A sudden transformation from cooperative colleague and respected associate to office tyrant and budget curmudgeon is a credibility killer. Straight talk and plain dealing in meetings, hallway conversations, and one-on-one discussions is critical.

1. Aristotle, www.houseofquotes.com

Furthermore, develop a leadership style that best fits you. Do not misrepresent yourself by polishing someone else's ill-fitting, hand-me-down style. Adopt an approach that's uniquely "you." Start with exemplar leadership traits you noted over the years in others and deliberately cast off those less than effective examples as mistakes you will not repeat (see "Boss vs Leader"). Trust your intuition and lead your team in the way that naturally works for you as long as it meets the expectations of your boss.

Next, ensure words fully align with action because inconsistent action contradicts the spoken word, no matter how eloquently delivered. Credibility slips with each misplaced promise or broken pledge. Prevent an unintended downward credibility spiral by committing only to realistic deliverables.

Take timely action where appropriate but don't over commit. For example, promising jobholders a new CAD system, additional head-count, or "all the overtime you can handle" is a set up unless you are both the decision-maker and check writer. In America's frontier days, a cowpoke's spoken word was contract and his handshake the signature. Today's jobholders expect the same assurance.

Also, watch out for more subtle messages of commitment that jeopardize credibility. If you agree to "look into" an issue, follow-up—even if no action can be taken. Jobholders become frustrated when their issue drops from your radar screen.

Speak well of your direct reports especially with higher officials. This also demonstrates respect for jobholders and word of your flattering comments invariably circles back to enhance your credibility and leadership stature.

Be courteous and respectful in all dealings and especially vigilant when administering policies or resolving staff conflict. Respond promptly to complaints and suggestions and do not arbitrarily deny reasonable requests. Back up your direct reports too by defending them against unfair attack, interference, or intrusion, especially from above.

Appreciate that co-workers have lives away from their jobs that do impact work. Maintain human values in the workplace even under pressure to deliver results at any cost. Encourage life balance among the staff.

A great way to show jobholder respect and earn credibility is to expunge the secrecy culture. E9-1-1 dispatching is one tough job, requiring a special skill set and temperament that is often unappreciated. Show respect by sharing important information. This also builds a climate and culture of trust, which is needed when the news is significant or jobs are vulnerable. For example, jobholders appreciate knowing immediately both the "why" and "when" relative to proposed changes in their work shift (eight to twelve hours), on-the-job benefits (cut-rate medical insurance), or a merger/consolidation (with attendant reduction-in-force).

If jobholders can't get timely and accurate information from their supervisor, they typically learn about issues through inaccurate or out-dated rumors. Moreover, sharing important information early and often demonstrates your respect for the collective job maturity of the staff—a credibility enhancer indeed.

Finally, lead by example. Convey integrity, enthusiasm, and pride in your on-the-job performance, professionalism, and initiative—this includes "just being around." The absentee supervisor who "works from home" or when in the office, arrives late, keeps the office door closed, and then leaves early sets an awful leadership example which can quickly become a contagion.

INSTITUTE PERFORMANCE EXPECTATIONS[2]

Written workplace expectations fuel performance and desirable on-the-job behaviors by reducing jobholders' frustration and discontent. Formal performance expectations provide both guidance and responsibility for specific, achievable goals vital to the success of the Communications Center. Written performance expectations go beyond job descriptions and address priorities, attitudes, and behaviors indispensable to this success. This "road map" contains unambiguous indicators of what constitutes good, better, and best performance, which eliminates guesswork about how success is defined, measured, and reviewed. Expectations create multiple opportunities for the jobholder to succeed while building a win-win working partnership between you and jobholders.

Expectations also serve as the benchmark to accurately and fairly assess performance. Without clear expectations, jobholders can only guess at what it means to do a "good" job. Moreover, without expectations you are aiming at a moving target when preparing the written performance review. When meaningful and credible expectations are measured against results and a clear-cut performance standard, your credibility is enhanced and jobholders seldom use the word "unfair." Consider introducing written expectations early in either individual 1:1 meetings with direct reports or at one of your first formal staff

2. Performance expectations or minimum core competencies are generic attributes, characteristics, or behaviors that are not explicitly part of a profession's core of knowledge or technical skills but are nevertheless required for job success.

meetings. Place a signed copy in the jobholder's official HR file, and provide jobholders with one for reference.

DO NOT ACQUIESCE TO THE CURRENT WAY OF DOING BUSINESS

The Communications Center challenge is to keep co-workers constructively focused on important tasks and the Center's life-saving mission. So, break the cycle of constricting bureaucracy, mindless process, and meaningless paperwork—all of which zap productivity. Examine questionable policies and procedures, and then eliminate distracting and frustrating administrative and structural interference.[3] This credibility enhancer will immediately win the hearts and minds of co-workers and is the benchmark of a progressive and decisive leader. Strive also to establish a unique momentum and fast-paced culture for work in the unit.

MAKE AN IMMEDIATE DIFFERENCE

The title of "supervisor" is bestowed upon the position holder who earns their stripes through effective supervisory leadership. Take charge and make informed decisions early in your tenure. Consider eliminating irritants such as reserved parking spaces for "essential personnel only" (are we not all essential?) or special privileges such as overtime for the chosen few. These are "command decisions" with little down side.

However, chose wisely which administrative battles to fight.[4] Research current issues, and then display common sense by making informed decisions, but in a timely manner. Do not act unilaterally unless time is critical or an emergency arises. Do your homework, solicit input, and ask others for their "read" of the situation.

Demonstrate competent leadership, especially through timely decisions, but do more than just make cosmetic changes—make the right changes. Correct problems quickly, especially performance- and

3. Interference is intrinsically related to overall performance by this formula:
    $JPC=(T - I) \times A2$ where
    JP=Jobholder Performance Capacity
    T=Talent (Skills, Knowledge, Ability)
    I=Interference
    A2=Attitude squared
4. For an excellent read on this topic, see Sun Tzu (1971) *The Art of War*, translated with a forward by Samuel B. Griffith, Oxford University Press, chapter 5.

morale-impacting issues, and start rewarding positive behavior imme-diately. Providing recognition for work well done rewards behavior you want emulated and repeated.

Make jobholder heroes by developing "go to" people or subject matter experts (SME). Morale is typically high on a police department SWAT team or fire department Haz-Mat team for just this reason. We all enjoy being viewed as a unique someone with a special skill set and singular competency. Harness the collective genius of your Communications Center through SMEs and watch morale go up and "eliteness" coalesce.[5]

DO NOT UNDERVALUE ADMINISTRATIVE TASKS

Enhance your credibility by completing important administrative tasks on or ahead of schedule. This is particularly critical for performance reviews especially when a pay raise is involved. Sign off on expense reports and approve overtime quickly. Missing a payroll deadline for a salary increase or expense reimbursement is a bona fide morale buster.

Another undervalued administrative task with a big credibility pay-off is 1:1 meetings with each direct report. Conducted on a regular basis, jobholders look forward to this exclusive time with "the boss." Moreover, the perceptive supervisor will learn about bothersome issues and the strengths, weaknesses, and interests of each jobholder during these special meetings. This is also a good time to underscore Communications Center expectations, assess progress on assigned goals, and discuss career development.

EMPHASIZE TRAINING AND CONTINUOUS IMPROVEMENT

Competent supervisors ensure the Communications Center runs smoothly under all conditions even when not there. Leadership by example coupled with realistic training ensures jobholders will step up in an emergency with the same confident, even-tempered demeanor as you would. Meaningful training displaces "crisis-management" with composed, analytical problem-solvers you developed. Comprehensive training about unusual events and upcoming technologies like a new

---

5. At a recent staff meeting here at Intrado Inc., each SME received a professionally framed "diploma" (similar to a college degree) illuminating their unique SME title and special duties "together with all the honors, rights, and duties belonging thereto. In testimony whereof, this seal and signature as authorized by the Business Unit Vice-President and Director are hereto affixed."

CAD or radio system translates into a calm reaction by all when the real event occurs or the switch is thrown on the new system.

Effective supervisors also strive for continuous improvement (CI) in operations and administration. CI means the Communications Center's collective expertise progressively increases each month along with the performance bar.

In sum, successful supervisory leadership is a function of establishing and maintaining professional credibility. By avoiding common mistakes and following a few lessons learned from others, an incoming Communications Center Supervisor can enjoy a long and rewarding tenure.

MISTAKES TO AVOID WHEN TAKING OVER AS COMMUNICATIONS CENTER SUPERVISOR

- Fail to lead by example.
- Fail to support/defend staff.
- Fail to make training a priority.
- Fail to improve operations continuously.
- Fail to reward performance.
- Fail to enrich jobs.
- Use consistently bad judgment.
- Dither on the unimportant.
- Show no interest in the technical side.
- Fail to set expectations.
- Be inconsistent when applying policy.
- Panic during emergencies.
- Fight silly battles.
- Fail to deliver on promises.
- Become invisible.

KEYS TO ESTABLISHING YOUR COMMUNICATIONS CENTER AS SOMEPLACE SPECIAL[6]

Goal	*Enabling Objective*
1. Take conspicuous pride in your work/job.	✔ Strive ceaselessly for excellence; lead/inspire by personal example.

6. See "Someplace Special: Subtle Steps to Building a Super Loyal Staff", Executive Strategies, National Institute of Business Management, September 4, 1990.

2. Promote a friendly atmosphere.

3. Share rewards and recognition.

4. Provide rewards that exceed expectations.

5. Recognize individuals and individual talent.

6. Show how every individual fits in and contributes.

7. Set a distinctive style and workplace tone.

8. Promote job enrichment.

9. Build an atmosphere of trust.

10. Appreciate attitudes not just results.

✔ Make openness part of the culture.

✔ Send high-level accolades downstream to "operations."

✔ Bump up rewards in quality/cost; reward desirable behaviors.

✔ Use first names; know on-the-job talents and off-the-job interests.

✔ Show up/downstream work linkages and each position's value-add.

✔ Demonstrate your team's signature "eliteness" via attitude and actions.

✔ Delegate; develop Subject Matter Experts; career path jobholders.

✔ Share information; respect confidences; disdain gossip; reward performance.

✔ Ensure results are tempered with collegiality and civil discourse.

Boss	*Leader*
✔ "Read my lips"	✔ "Read my record"
✔ Takes credit	✔ Takes charge
✔ Lets stuff happen	✔ Makes stuff happen
✔ Talk	✔ Action
✔ Gatekeeper	✔ Keeper of the flame
✔ Caretaker	✔ Caregiver
✔ Needs recognition	✔ Gives recognition
✔ Enjoys class distinctions	✔ Eliminates class distinctions
✔ Anesthetized mediocrity	✔ "Center of Excellence"
✔ Makes administrative decisions	✔ Makes strategic decisions
✔ The clock matters	✔ Craftsmanship matters
✔ "Know it all"	✔ Applied intelligence
✔ Moving performance targets	✔ Written expectations
✔ "No one knows"	✔ "Let's find out"
✔ Makes promises	✔ Fulfills commitments

✔ Encourages office politics
✔ A marginal example
✔ Ditherer
✔ Has good intentions
✔ Subjective Umpire
✔ Reclusive
✔ Unilateral
✔ Team of one
✔ Thin skinned
✔ Consumes resources
✔ Intractable lineman
✔ Shakes confidence
✔ "Get here on time"
✔ Problem creator
✔ Remedial mechanic
✔ Suspicious
✔ Affixes blame
✔ "Go!"
✔ Face time
✔ Tough on people
✔ Impersonal
✔ Status quo

✔ Stodgy bureaucrat
✔ Creates headwinds
✔ Hoards information

✔ Disdains silliness
✔ Leads by example
✔ Capacity of boldness
✔ Creates reality
✔ Objective mediator
✔ Approachable
✔ Collaborative
✔ Player/Coach
✔ Deploys under fire
✔ Provides resources
✔ Selfless blocking back
✔ Instills self-confidence
✔ Arrives ahead of time
✔ Problem eliminator
✔ Tune-up specialist
✔ Trusting
✔ Fixes root cause
✔ "Let's go!"
✔ Results
✔ Tough on workplace values
✔ Interpersonal
✔ Culture of Continuous
  Improvement
✔ Nonwork eliminator
✔ Removes structural roadblocks
✔ Shares key information

COMMUNICATIONS CENTER ADVICE

▪ Above all else, recruit/retain good people.
▪ Believe in Disney's First Law. "If you can dream it, you can do it."
▪ Envision a "Center of E9-1-1 Excellence."
▪ Communicate your "excellence" blueprint and the endgame.
▪ Remain focused on the Communications Center's basic purpose and mission.
▪ Trust jobholders to apply their talent to solve problems and make important decisions.
▪ Celebrate when magic happens.
▪ Make heroes of your good people.

The Mentor/Protégé Relationship:
Fostering the Development of the
Next Generation of Telecommunicators

by:
JOE SCHUMACHER
SSN 525-78-7466
Director, Data Integrity Unit, Intrado Inc., Boulder, Colorado

and
JIMMYE O'CONNOR
SSN 128-34-4490
Senior Data Analyst and Mentor Program Coordinator
Intrado Inc., Boulder, Colorado

This article explores the Mentor/Protégé relationship within the unique context of an emergency communications center. Also examined are roles and expectations, mentoring tips and techniques, as well as the merits of participating as a Mentor. Several sidebars are included, along with an informal sample Mentor/Protégé "agreement."

Some training programs operate under a tight budget and abbreviated schedules because the new hire is needed "ASAP" to fill a critical shift shortage and/or to reduce overtime. With much to learn and little time for comprehensive hands-on practice, a formal Mentor/Protégé relationship (we prefer Protégé over "trainee") provides both supplemental and extended training during an abridged classroom-to-real-world transition. Under a Mentor's constant guardianship, the new hire can be quickly placed "on line" without undue liability or compromising public safety.

THE MENTOR/PROTÉGÉ RELATIONSHIP(S)

Mentorship is a deliberate adult-to-adult learning partnership between an experienced and inexperienced person. This formal "in-house" process is designed to nurture and grow talent. The Mentor demonstrates, explains, and models while the Protégé observes, questions, and explores. The Mentor's obvious charge is to cross-pollinate by developing the Protégé's on-the-job skill set. The Mentor accomplishes this by sharing his or her valuable time and priceless operational expertise. Overall, the Mentor supports and challenges the Protégé by teaching, guiding, advising, counseling, sponsoring, role modeling, validating, motivating, protecting, and communicating in a setting of reciprocal trust and mutual respect. Equally as important, the seasoned Mentor crafts a safe and secure environment for the Protégé to thrive.

"Old hand" Mentors know that camaraderie and friendship are a vital component of successful Mentoring. Seasoned Mentors strive to eliminate the 'sink or swim' mindset a new hire might experience while at the same time maintaining constant vigilance for signs that the Protégé may be struggling, feeling overwhelmed and becoming disenfranchised. Using expressions such as, "I had a similar experience during my training" or "I had trouble grasping that concept too" validates the Protégé's feelings, creates a bond, and places them at ease. This reduces the likelihood of the protégé disconnecting and then departing in frustration during or immediately after expensive and time-consuming training.

The Mentor knows that helping the Protégé build a sense of personal competence, a feeling of self-worth, and the knowledge, skill, and ability to make informed decisions can be more important than the Mentor's sharing of operational knowledge or technical matter expertise. The goal of formal Mentorship is to produce a Protégé who becomes a vested shareholder in the communication center's successful operations.

So, Mentorship couples classroom theory with real-world experience and hands-on activity to develop the Protégé's critical job skill set. By building "craft skills" under the attentive eye of the seasoned "elder", the Protégé is exposed to practical "know-how" that can only be acquired with "journeyman" guidance, hands-on application, and "fail safe" experimentation. The Mentor and Protégé must therefore enter into a skill transfer partnership (see Sidebar 3, "Informal Mentorship Agreement", p. 175) concentrating on an array of intrinsic and practical skills assembled by the Mentor from both classroom and accumulated practical experience. The Protégé transforms classroom knowledge into practical expertise via application in the context and actual setting in which the newly acquired knowledge and skills are to be used. This hands-on experience is essential to the Protégé's long-term on-the-job success.

Accomplished Mentors use different developmental techniques throughout the Mentorship period. Initially, the Mentor might introduce the Protégé to simple processes and procedures through shadowing or a "sit-along." Then, when the Protégé is comfortable and prepared to apply their new skill set, they participate in a critical trial-and-error period allowing experimentation with minimum risk. The Protégé learns by modeling proven problem-solving strategies while articulating his or her thought processes. The veteran Mentor begins to decrease assistance gradually, while constantly asking open-ended questions such as, "What should you do next?" During this time, the Mentor provides pointers and advice while the Protégé explains his or her decisions. At this important stage, the Mentor's goal is to develop know-how and encourage self-confidence, not necessarily to solve the applied problem for the Protégé.

A typical sequence might start with a brief overview including asking why the task is important, explaining how the task is accomplished, and where and how the task fits into the "big picture." The Mentor then demonstrates the task while taking the Protégé through each step including accessing reference manuals or documented work instructions. The Protégé is then asked to state his or her understanding of the task and allowed to walk through the task while applying new skills. At this point the Protégé should "go it alone" with the Mentor offering help only when asked. Once the Protégé has demonstrated the essential behavior, the task is repeated. The experienced Mentor knows that "over-learning" is critical to second nature recall under the stressful conditions of "live" action. Industrial psychologists say this is developing the thinking skills and frames of reference for sequential and progressive application.

MANAGING ROLES AND PERFORMANCE EXPECTATIONS

A formal "code of practice," or written expectations, helps both the Mentor and Protégé navigate this special partnership (see Sidebars, pp. 173–75). Thus, addressing expectations should be an absolute day-one activity and is the best time to set clear conduct boundaries and workaday ground rules. A list of expectations reduces the likelihood of unpleasant surprises and unanticipated problems on both sides, thus eliminating the ubiquitous "I just didn't know" Protégé response.

Mentoring is most successful when the Protégé trusts the Mentor, feels accepted and views the Mentor as a role model. Therefore, shared trust and mutual respect are the foundation for a successful relationship and learning environment. The paramount expectation is, correspondingly, that the Protégé may be trusted with restricted or confidential information. Any breech of confidence or violation of trust sends a silver bullet through the Protégé's credibility. Hence, the Protégé is expected to keep all information strictly confidential unless otherwise specified. The fire service rule for medical emergencies is applicable here: "What you say, hear, and do on the job stays on the job."

Additionally, the Protégé should expect frequent and regular feedback in the form of candid performance assessments. It's human nature to be sensitive to unduly harsh criticism. However, a Protégé with high job-maturity will value constructive information and valid performance comments, if fair yet firmly delivered, as a mechanism for rapid improvement. "Touch points" or a regularly scheduled candid exchange to critically evaluate progress and output brings about desired results. When a Protégé successfully demonstrates mastery of a new skill, he or she has taken responsibility for their development. The experienced Mentor actually creates "opportunities" for the Protégé to demonstrate success when feedback is immediate. "Catch 'em doing something right" is the veteran Mentor's motto along with regularly celebrating successes. Other important expectations can be found in Sidebar 3, "What the Mentor Expects of the Protégé."

THE MERITS OF MENTORING

The essence of leadership is indeed lifelong learning and the teaching of others. Accordingly, Mentorship quickly identifies emerging leaders among telecommunicators by providing an opportunity for them to showcase their teaching, leading, and counseling skills. Thus, the demonstrated mindset and workaday conduct along with the professional goals and aspirations of the Mentor, can be subsequently reflected in the Protégé. Moreover, through the teaching process, the Mentor also upgrades his or her own knowledge, skills, and ability. Invariably, a protégé will ask a technical or procedural question that stumps the Mentor. Seasoned instructors can also attest that the fastest way to master a given topic is to teach it to someone else. Topic research, along with preparation and delivery either formally in the classroom or informally side-by-side with the new telecommunicator, hones public speaking and people-development skills as well. These are essential components to develop and showcase for aspiring Supervisors and Managers. Equally important, Mentoring is prestigious.

Selection as a Mentor within the Emergency Telecommunications Center should be a high honor accompanied by public recognition of technical competence and validation of knowledge, skills, and ability. Correspondingly, selection as a Mentor provides increased peer recognition and self-esteem. Becoming a Mentor can increase an employee's motivation by providing a career challenge along with exposing them to new insights and perspectives resulting in a unique opportunity for self-development. Mentoring is also a great opportunity to positively influence the next generation of telecommunicators. A Mentor is often judged by the subsequent performance of the Protégé, so the impact of Mentoring could, indeed, last a lifetime and save a life.

When a former Protégé serves as a Mentor, he or she "pays back" the organization for the training and Mentoring received, which at the time probably reduced stress, made a friend, and shortened the learning curve while increasing job satisfaction, loyalty, and productivity. Mentoring returns with compound interest the gifts of knowledge, learning, advice, feedback, focus, and support.

In summary, Mentorship is the critical link between the didactic classroom and real-world application. A trusted, patient, committed, and understanding Mentor provides the vital hands-on training needed to endow the Protégé with knowledge to perform critical tasks, processes, and specific work instructions—some of which may not be documented. Especially effective during the training cycle, a Mentor provides a context in which knowledge and skills just acquired in the minds-on classroom can be incorporated straightaway via hands-on application in the emergency communications center. Most importantly, the Mentor provides performance support for his Protégé during the critical transition period in the form of assistance with daily tasks, developing a skill set, as well as communicating the organization's corporate culture, social infrastructure, workaday values, and performance expectations.

The end result is a Protégé who feels welcome and perceives him/herself as being a valued part of an exciting collaborative partnership of professional telecommunicators. The mentored Protégé is more relaxed and comfortable and learns job tasks more rapidly and thoroughly. Thus, the newly graduated telecommunicator is a credit to him/herself, the Communications Center, the organization, the community, and just as importantly, the Mentor.

SIDEBAR 1: CHARACTERISTICS OF A GOOD MENTOR

- Has strong interpersonal skills—can easily talk and listen to people.
- Has demonstrated coaching, counseling, and facilitating skills.
- Believes that people want to learn.
- Displays personal power and high self-esteem.
- Has state-of-the-art technical knowledge.
- Has positive experiences to share.
- Has a good reputation for helping others and developing skills.
- Has the time and mental energy to devote to the relationship.

- Has a vested interest in the profession and the organization's mission.

SIDEBAR 2: WHAT THE PROTÉGÉ EXPECTS OF THE MENTOR

- Lead by example: be a role model and collaborative learning partner.
- Define expectations and work rules.
- Impart values and high standards for on-the-job behavior.
- Build mutual trust.
- Be a sounding board and friendly ear, listening with both intuition and heart.
- Be an approachable friend, advocate, support structure, and professional advisor.
- Supervise work efforts.
- Communicate frequently, openly, and candidly.
- Mutually formulate challenging but attainable goals.
- Be readily available and approachable (even under a high workload).
- Be fair and consistent.
- Provide opportunities for challenge and growth.
- Be an information/resource provider.
- Be a technical-matter expert, share stories, and institutional memory.
- Treat the Protégé as a colleague, not a trainee or fraternity pledge.
- Do not take advantage of the Protégé.

SIDEBAR 3: WHAT THE MENTOR EXPECTS OF THE PROTÉGÉ

- Keep information confidential.
- Ask for help and ask questions!
- Share frustrations.
- Display a high degree of job maturity.
- Commit to the rigorous training regime and to expand capabilities.
- Display an interest and curiosity in all aspects of the challenging job.
- Demonstrate a sound work ethic and commitment to the values of the organization.
- Complete all assigned tasks on time.
- Communicate in a civil and collegial manner.
- Work cooperatively with others.
- Adopt and follow through on performance improvement recommendations.
- Be open and receptive to new ways and ideas.

- Focus on results.
- Possess a sense of personal responsibility.
- Manage both time and projects.
- Set priorities.
- Make no excuses.

INFORMAL MENTORSHIP AGREEMENT

We, _____, the Mentor and _____, the Protégé, commit to this Mentoring relationship within the _____Telecommunications Center. In addition, we agree to the following:

ß   To maintain this Mentor relationship beginning __/__/__ and ending by mutual consent of the Mentor and Supervisor.
ß   To maintain contact of approximately _____ hour/s daily.
ß   To work towards achieving these professional goals:

1. _____
2. _____
3. _____
4. _____
5. _____

We fully understand the guidelines for Mentoring relationships, including upholding the confidentiality of information learned and to respect each other's roles and formal positions. By signing below, we accept the above guidelines.

_____

MENTOR SIGNATURE   DATE

_____

PROTÉGÉ SIGNATURE   DATE

The following were present at the signing of this agreement. Each party agrees to assist/support this relationship.

_____

SIGNATURE   DATE

_____

SIGNATURE   DATE

Fostering a Culture of Partnership, Performance, and Accountability Through Winning Expectations

An 800-word article prepared for:

SONYA CARIUS
Editor, 911 News
422 Beecher Rd., Columbus, OH 43230, sonya@nena9-1-1.org

by:
JOE SCHUMACHER
Director, Texas Operations, Intrado Inc., Boulder, Colorado
jschumacher@Intrado.com

and
TERI DEPUY
Senior Vice-President, Organizational Development
Intrado Inc., Boulder, Colorado, tdepuy@Intrado.com

Teri DePuy is the Senior Vice-president of organizational development for Intrado Inc. of Longmont, Colorado. Her leadership experience at Intrado includes contributions in operations, training, project management, and complex data services. Prior to joining Intrado Inc., Teri had over ten years experience in the public sector including dispatch supervisor and the training manager for the Boulder Regional Communications Center (BRCC). Teri is a certified Emergency Number Professional (ENP) through NENA.

FOSTERING A CULTURE OF PARTNERSHIP, PERFORMANCE, AND ACCOUNTABILITY THROUGH WINNING EXPECTATIONS

Performance expectations or minimum core competencies are generic attributes, characteristics, or behaviors that are not explicitly part of a profession's core of knowledge or technical skills but are nevertheless required for job success. Setting these expectations logically begins with a review of each direct report's job description. Simple or core employer expectations might include making a good first impression, staying informed of workplace rules, maintaining a positive attitude, demonstrating timeliness in attendance and assignment completion, keeping supervisors informed, asking questions, doing a good job, wearing proper attire, working safely, scheduling time off, admitting mistakes, respecting others, keeping personal telephone usage to a minimum, and using all company resources wisely.

However, winning performance expectations go beyond the job description by addressing the overall priorities, attitudes, and behaviors indispensable to success for the jobholder.[1] Winning expectations lay the foundation for a collaborative partnership between manager and jobholder since unambiguous indicators of what constitutes good, better, and best criteria are identified and acknowledged early in the relationship. Taken in total, winning performance expectations foster a culture of partnership, accountability, and productivity.

Because it is easier to create more of "something" when that "something" is clearly defined, written expectations eliminate the guesswork about performance metrics or how success is defined. Concise, detailed, and specific expectations, communicated with exacting priorities, desired outcomes, and precise deadlines assist the job holder in understanding the scope of behaviors, knowledge, skills, values, and attitudes expected of them. Hence, expectations become the jobholder's guiding framework to mastering the job and understanding what it takes to be "successful." No doubt you've heard the managerial proverb "What gets measured, gets done." Like a first-rate roadmap, expectations keep the jobholder's attention focused on the desired destination—whether it be completing a task, producing a desired output, or meeting a deadline.

As importantly, winning expectations serve as the manager's benchmark to accurately and fairly assessing performance.[2] For example, many managers rank writing an annual performance review and convening the related meeting somewhere between a root canal and completing income tax forms. However, assessing performance is a daily and inescapable part of every manager's job, and a contributing factor for this unpleasantness is the lack of written performance expectations for each job cluster. Without clear expectations, jobholders can only guess at what it means to do a "good" job while the evaluating manager aims for a moving target when formally assessing performance. When meaningful and credible expectations are measured

1. See Sidebar "Intrado Managers' Expectations."
2. See Sidebar "Types of Expectations/Performance Metrics."

against results and a clear-cut performance standard, gaps are easily identified and corrective action promptly taken. Winning expectations illuminate the variance between target results and actual performance.

An ongoing discussion throughout the year of the jobholder's performance–to include knowledge, skill, ability, attitude, teamwork, etc.–is a vital aspect of every manager's job. Moreover, this process has a significant influence on the collective performance and productivity of the entire work unit. For example, expectations-based performance reviews are the optimal instrument to:

- Attain the organization's mission, goals, and objectives.
- Inform the jobholder of strengths, weaknesses, and progress.
- Strengthen the work relationships and improve communication between manager and jobholder.
- Develop jobholder skills.
- Recognize accomplishments including good, better, and best work.
- Recommend employees for merit increases, promotions, and other rewards.

Key milestones in the jobholder's employment, such as new hire orientation, individual meetings, and performance reviews, are additional opportunities to introduce–then continually underscore–core performance expectations. Within these forums the entire workforce learns one-by-one of the organization's core values and expected behaviors. When communicated and reinforced, written expectations become the new norm and organizational infrastructure.

During the new hire orientation, for example, performance expectations should be discussed with the jobholder. A signed copy should then be placed in his or her official HR personnel file, with another provided to the jobholder for daily reference. Another opportunity is via feedback during private discussions. Most experts agree that performance feedback should be regular and ongoing. Thus, a monthly one-on-one meeting with each direct report is an optimal time to provide performance feedback and underscore expectations. This also keeps the conversation focused on behavior and not personal attributes.

Gen X employees, described as being more inquisitive about why "things" happen, tend to seek a higher order of organizational involvement. Conversely, they are impatient with bureaucratic silliness and stuffy traditional hierarchies (sound like all jobholders?). Established workplace expectations fuel performance by reducing jobholders' frustration and discontent. Formal performance expectations provide both guidance and responsibility for specific, achievable goals, and inclusion in organizational success.

Managers at all levels are responsible for defining expectations, contributing to organizational performance and upholding the corporate culture. Therefore, expectations should be clearly espoused in the organization's vision and values statements, documented in job descriptions and job postings, and articulated to employees during career planning and development discussions.

In sum, how jobholders and consequently the organization collectively perform depends on how unambiguously acceptable behavior is defined. Clear expectations contribute to high productivity and low turnover while hazy expectations result in low performance and high turnover. Expectations create multiple opportunities for the jobholder to succeed while building a win-win working partnership between the manager and jobholder. Thus when properly led, ordinary people achieve extraordinary results.

SIDEBAR 1: INTRADO MANAGERS' EXPECTATIONS

High-quality Communications

- Conduct regular staff meetings with direct reports—preference is weekly.
- Conduct regular one-on-one meetings with direct reports—preference is quarterly.
- Review the job description and expectations with each employee periodically.
- Provide regular status updates (v-mail or e-mail) on escalations.
- Submit weekly status reports on time.
- Document all formal customer meetings via written minutes to track key decisions and action items.

Performance Reviews

- Provide mentor feedback in writing, once a month for the first six months, where a formal mentoring relationship is in place.
- Complete annual reviews on time.
- Keep employee working files to document performance throughout the review period.
- Use as a forum for goal setting, career-path definition, and exploring new opportunities.
- Ensure that merit increases follow Human Resources best practices.
- Provide ongoing, direct, honest, and timely feedback to employees.

Employee Recognition

- Celebrate achievements and performance milestones.
- Announce and recognize all promotions.
- Say "thank you" frequently and publicly.
- Be creative with appreciation events.

Role Model Corporate Values and Work Ethics

- Position yourself as the leader through actions; demonstrate integrity as a core value.
- Be a team player, i.e. use your own authority to achieve accomplishments, not "the boss wants..."
- Practice zero tolerance for office politics, backbiting, and behind-the-scenes criticism of peers.
- Practice courtesy, professionalism, and respect (CPR).
- Support the organization's vision and mission.

Leadership

- Demonstrate poise, confidence, and decisiveness.
- Be knowledgeable and well-informed.
- Encourage reasonable risk-taking in decision making.
- Create cross-functional work teams to empower employees to make decisions/recommendations and define solutions.
- Encourage collaborative decision making with jobholders vs only top-down decision making.
- Hold jobholders accountable and track completion dates.
- Develop trust and effective working relationships with peers across organizational boundaries.

Personal and Professional Development

- Partner and employee management: do your part in each role.
- Attend and encourage (or require) staff to participate in company-sponsored training courses.
- Participate in and support industry organizations and standards bodies.
- Encourage outside activities and participation in civic events.
- Participate in company-sponsored programs.
- Embrace opportunities to conduct presentations or training courses.

Fiscal Responsibilities

- Create realistic and accurate expense budgets on time.
- Reconcile monthly expense reports and resolve discrepancies.
- Maintain an organized expense tracking system.
- Monitor and adhere to signature authority and purchasing guidelines.

Safety and Security Measures

Take immediate and appropriate corrective action and document:

- Incidents or innuendoes related to sexual harassment.
- Incidents or innuendoes related to diversity matters.
- Incidents or actions that could jeopardize employee safety.
- Incidents or actions that could compromise the security of intellectual property, the personal safety of employees, or company property.

Succession Planning

- Develop a successor.
- Mentor staff into positions of leadership.
- Delegate appropriately.
- Create opportunities for individuals to lead and make decisions.

Acknowledge receipt:

_____   _____

Name   Date

SIDEBAR 2: TYPES OF EXPECTATION/PERFORMANCE METRICS

Threshold

Definition: A particular value is derived analytically or intuitively that defines the minimally acceptable value of the measure that will enable the work unit to be successful. Example: The Telephone Service Provider (TSP) prefers 95% data accuracy before "cut over" for any new Countywide enhanced 9-1-1 services. The County's addressing unit will meet that performance level before going "live."

Baseline

Definition: Data has previously been collected over time using the same measurement process. To be considered successful, the current results must exceed the results obtained during a comparable period earlier in time.

Example: Police Department average response time to emergency calls last quarter was 5:30 minutes; this quarter the PD will improve on this time by 20%.

Target

Definition: A particular value is derived analytically or intuitively that states some desired ultimate value of the measure that will enable the work unit to be successful.

Example: The targeted 9-1-1 public education program will continue until a 50% reduction rate in after-school crank 9-1-1 calls is achieved.

Benchmark

Definition: Results using the same measurement process for either a comparable work unit or an exemplary work unit is available. To be considered successful, the current results must either exceed or attain a particular proportion of that benchmark.

Example: The industry "best practice" for use of EMD protocols on first-aid emergency call is 80%; this communications center shall attain that value.

Bibliography

Bohm, David, *On Dialogue,* Routledge, 1996

Branden, Nathaniel, *The Six Pillars of Self-Esteem*, Bantam, 1995

Capra, Fritjof, *The Turning Point*, Bantam Books, 1988

Chopra, Deepak, *The Conscious Universe,* Hay House Audio, 2000

Covey, Stephen R., *The 7 Habits of Highly Effective People*, Simon and Schuster, 1990

Deaton, Dennis R., *The Book on Mind Management*, MMI Publishing, 1996

Greenleaf, Robert K., *Servant Leadership*, Paulist Press, 1977

Gribbin, John, *In Search of Schrodinger's Cat*, Bantam Books, 1984

Ipsaro, Anthony J., Ph.D., Psy.D. *White Men, Women and Minorities in the Changing Work Force,* Meridian Associates, 1997

Jaworski, Joseph, *Synchronicity: The Inner Path of Leadership*, Berrett-Koehler, 1996

Lewin, Roger, *Complexity*, University of Chicago Press, 1999

Lovelock, James, *Gaia*, Oxford, 1990

Maturana, Humberto R. and Francisco J. Varela, *The Tree of Knowledge*, Shambhala Publications, Inc., 1987

McMaster, Michael D., The Intelligence Advantage, Butterworth–Heinemann, 1996

Siler, Todd, *Breaking the Mind Barrier*, Simon and Schuster, 1990

Siler, Todd, *Think Like A Genius*, Bantam Books, 1997

Waldrop, M. Mitchell, *Complexity: The Emerging Science at the Edge of Order and Chaos*, Simon and Schuster, 1993

Wheatley, Margaret J., *Leadership and the New Science,* Berrett-Koehler, 1999

Zohar, Dana, *Rewiring the Corporate Brain*, Berrett-Koehler, 1997

Zukov, Gary, *The Dancing Wu Li Masters*, Bantam Books, 1980

Index